How

Short Story

Competitions

Second Edition

How to Win

Short Story

Competitions

Second Edition

Dave Haslett & Geoff Nelder

ideas4writers

Table of Contents

About the authors

Dave Haslett [D] won his first writing competition at the age of seven and wrote his first book when he was thirteen. He founded ideas4writers in 2002 as an outlet for the thousands of writing ideas that filled his head but which he would never have the time to use. He has since released that collection as a series of 35 books.

His other books include *The Fastest Way to Write Your Book* and *The Fastest Way to Get Ideas*. He has organised and judged two ideas4writers short story competitions, each of which attracted hundreds of entries.

Geoff Nelder [G] is a former teacher who is now the British editor for Adventure Books of Seattle, the publisher of novels and anthologies with a science fiction or adventure theme. He has read thousands of short story submissions for the science fiction anthologies at Adventure Books of Seattle, and wrote a critique for each one. He has entered many short story and novel competitions and has won or been highly placed in several. He was the short fiction judge for the Helen Whittaker Prize, and the 2018 judge for the FicFun international fiction contest. He has had seven novels, three non-fiction books and over 100 short stories published.

I've known Geoff for many years. He's a very good writer and joined my website, ideas4writers, within the first few weeks of it opening. He's been an active member ever since, always taking part in forum discussions, critiquing members' work, and passing on excellent advice. We've met a few times too, at various writing conferences, and our conversations – generally conducted in the bar, of course – have always been most enjoyable.

Having judged two ideas4writers short story competitions, I had a good idea of the most common mistakes people make. I even wrote a couple of articles on the subject. So when Geoff said he'd been appointed as that year's judge for the Whittaker Prize and had also judged the competition three years earlier, I leapt at the chance of picking his brain and turning my articles into something more substantial. Happily, Geoff relished the chance to pass on his knowledge. I knew he would!

Geoff caught a train down to where I live in "sunny" Devon and we went to the seaside. It was raining. So we installed ourselves in the hotel's dining room and chatted away for a few hours about short story competitions: pretty much everything we know about entering, judging and winning them. The whole thing was recorded, and this book is the result of that conversation: it's basically the transcript of the audio recording, but with a bit of editing. We hope you find it useful.

We were planning to release the audio recording too, but there was a lot of background noise in the dining room at times. We also found out afterwards that one of the microphones had malfunctioned, and it sounded as if we were speaking down a long tube!

1. Why do organisations run writing competitions?

[D] So, Geoff, let's start by talking about why magazines, websites and other organisations run writing competitions.

[G] In particular I can talk about the Whittaker Prize, which is a fairly new competition. It's been running since about 2006.

Many special interest group forums on the internet go through a life-cycle, and by the third or fourth year much of the interest has flagged. Even if it was meant to be a critique forum, you often find that the reading and analysis diminishes. One way to liven all of that up is to hold a competition.

In this case, the members of *The Write Idea* forum[1] suggested to the new owners that they could have a competition. It had to be quite a strict competition where there was a fee to enter, and there should be a cash prize at the end of it. Because it was a critique forum, they wanted feedback on their stories, and they wanted them scored.

One of the annoying things about some competitions is that you never get useful feedback. For *The Write Idea* forum members, the feedback was more important than winning. So *The Write Idea* organised the Whittaker competition and named it after the forum's founder, Helen Whittaker. She's a good writer herself.

For other companies and magazines, competitions can raise their profile and make people more aware of them.

[D] It gives the press and media a newsworthy reason to mention them that they might not otherwise have. That's certainly why we ran writing competitions at ideas4writers. We wanted that press attention. More specifically, we wanted to get the ideas4writers website mentioned in the writing magazines.

[G] That's right, and I remember John Ravenscroft won one of your competitions. He's a well-known short fiction writer, and it was good to see him at ideas4writers.

Competitions can raise funds and stimulate writing and creativity amongst the members of that organisation.

[D] Ours didn't raise funds; that was never the intention. We deliberately made them free-to-enter. But on the other hand, we didn't give feedback or critiques.

If we were to run another one, we would definitely offer feedback because we now realise how important it is. But there would obviously need to be an entry fee to cover the cost of doing that. In our case we wouldn't aim to profit from it, only to cover our costs, so it wouldn't be a fund-raising exercise. I know it can be that for other organisations. But what's more important for us is the publicity we get from running them, because that attracts new clients to the author services side of our business, and it increases the sales of our books.

[G] *The Write Idea* forum needed to raise funds, so charged a modest entry fee to pay for the competition prizes and the judges, and they also needed to raise enough to pay the internet fees and other costs of running the forum.

So that's the main reason why people run writing contests. They have to be masochistic to do it though, because it's a lot of hard work.

[D] Yes, it really is. I found that myself. It's a *huge* amount of work, and extremely time consuming. And that was without giving any feedback.

[G] Giving feedback *is* time-consuming, but I found it okay. The stories were 2,500 words or less, and it would take me about fifteen to twenty minutes to read them. Then it would take me another fifteen minutes to score them and write the feedback.

I'm used to writing feedback – I was a teacher for thirty years. In fact, for many years I taught every student in my school IT, which meant I had two projects from each of the two hundred pupils to grade every year, as well as many geography projects. I had to write teacher's reports, which before the days of ticklist LEA/computer reports required creativity. One fine example I pinched from another teacher: "The dawn of legibility in Kevin's handwriting sadly revealed his utter incapacity to spell."

Besides that, I used to be an editor on the BeWrite community forum. The forum doesn't exist any more, and BeWrite Books has closed down, but it was a fine literary small press publisher. I read and critiqued thousands of short stories on that, so I was used to critiquing.

Much of my critiquing technique was honed at a website called Café Doom[2], which is a serious critique group. It's mostly for horror and science fiction & fantasy writers. We used to do a lot of critiquing on that, and it's quite strict, well-coordinated and well-organised. Many of the members have been to Borderlands, which is an American critique organisation – it's like a boot camp for writers – and they've learnt the hard knock way of how to do critiquing. Some – including John Ravenscroft, for example – had been to the Alex Keegan boot camp, which was a tough British training ground for writers, but they came away as competition winners, as John showed.

[1] www.helenwhittaker.net/phpBB2
[2] www.cafedoom.com

2. Why writers should enter writing competitions

[D] What do you think writers get out of it if they win a competition? Apart from the prize money, of course.

[G] They win kudos, self-esteem, publicity for themselves and, most importantly, all writers should have a CV (curriculum vitae or résumé) and add their competition wins and runners-up. It's important.

[D] If you were entering a competition yourself, would you enter one that charged a fee but *didn't* give feedback?

[G] I might do now. All of my stories receive feedback because I belong to the critique groups I mentioned. If I have a story that I feel might stand a chance in a competition, I would know whether it has flaws in it according to the critiquers. So, yes, I *would* enter a competition now that didn't give feedback. But I encourage new writers to enter those that do.

[D] And are you in favour of entry fees?

[G] As a rule, I am, because it cuts out entries from people who aren't serious about their writing. Some entry fees are very high indeed, of course: we're talking about hundreds of pounds. That's tough, even for a prestigious competition, if you don't get any sort of feedback. I think that anyone who pays an entry fee, for any sort of competition, should have some feedback.

[D] If the competition you're entering doesn't give feedback, where else could you get it? You've mentioned online critique forums, for example. Which ones do you recommend?

[G] There are so many competitions that it won't be hard to find one that gives feedback. I recommend joining a writers' group as well. If you're lucky, your town will have a writers' circle you can join. Hopefully, it won't be "happy-clappy". Such groups will listen to you read your story and then they'll clap at the end of it. They don't say useful things like, "Ah, but you didn't use any colours in your story". It's sometimes painful to hear this, and you can cry a bit, but it's definitely what you need.

If you don't have a real-life writers' group in your town – or even if you do – join the many that are online. There's one called Critters[1], which is meant for science fiction and fantasy. If you do a web search for writers' critique groups you'll be swamped with a large number of them.

[D] Some feedback is going to be better than others, isn't it?

[G] That's right, yes. Some competitions insist that the judge writes a reasonable amount of feedback – I would say at least 50 words. At least one piece of feedback I wrote for the 2009 Whittaker Prize was as long as the story itself, but I got carried away and I felt that the writer deserved to have the analysis.

But I know there have been complaints in some competitions that the feedback is bizarre, or unfair, or written in a way that doesn't help the writer. For example, I know of a competition where the judge wrote things like, "The humour wasn't to my taste". Well, what does *that* mean? I think feedback has to be specific if it's going to be helpful.

[1] www.critters.org

[D] We've both been short story judges, though you've done it more recently than I have, and in much more depth. Could you describe what it feels like?

[G] It's a privilege, and an honour, to be able to read so many other people's ideas. After all, what I'm doing is sampling their heads, their imaginations.

I'm getting the benefit of all that – their best attempts at turning their imaginations into something worth reading and winning a competition. And I'm being paid to do it. Of course, it's hard work as well. I have to make the time to do all the reading, and writing the critiques, and making sure my critiques don't have any grammatical errors and that sort of thing – though I can't always guarantee that. But it was something I was pleased to do.

[D] And how did you become involved in judging competitions?

[G] Like any other jobs, I applied for them. As I mentioned earlier, the Whittaker competition is run by *The Write Idea*, which is a web-based forum for writers who aspire to literary excellence. They wanted judges for their 2009 competition, so they rushed out an advert that went to many literary sites. I thought, this is something I could be interested in. I knew the organisers – not that that gave me any favours – and I'd judged competitions before. Those competitions were also for short stories, but they were mostly horror, run by Eros and Rust from America. In this case, I was shortlisted, and then awarded the job.

The competition was run like most literary competitions, in that I didn't get to know who wrote what. The competitors sent their stories to the organisers, who cut off the names and any other clues about who wrote them, and then sent them to me via email. I read them by printing them off and taking them into my conservatory, or to a café somewhere, or sometimes putting them into my pannier and going off for a bike ride, and then reading them on a hillside or by the seaside. I like to be quite relaxed when I read them. I eventually read just over two hundred stories for that particular competition.

For the FicFun competition I was approached by the organisers. They said their researchers had seen that I'd judged competitions and they read some of my fiction and so wrote to invite me.

[D] Were you the only judge?

[G] For the Whittaker, I was the only fiction judge. There were two poetry judges as well. For FicFun I was the suspense fiction judge. Someone else judged the romance category.

It was easier for me to be the only judge for a category, and it saved a lot of time, not having to go to and fro between another judge. It also meant we didn't have to create a shortlist, because I was just scoring the stories. I was scoring them on various aspects, which I'll talk about in a moment.

It was hard work for me, but even more so for the competitors. For the Whittaker there were nine rounds, each two weeks apart. So at the end of it, if they did all nine rounds, each writer had nine stories they could use. They weren't obliged to enter something for every round, but most of them did.

[D] They each wrote *nine* separate stories?

[G] Yes. They were of mixed genre – any genre was acceptable. They had to have a maximum of 2,500 words. That was pretty much the only strict rule. If they went over 2,500 words they were disqualified. Sometimes I was asked by the organisers, "Hey, Geoff, this story seems to be 2,505 words, can you count it with *your* software and see if it's any different?"

[D] So if they went over by as few as five words they'd be disqualified?

[G] Yes, they would have been disqualified, but in fact none were. Some of them were spot-on the 2,500.

TIP: keep within the word count limit.

I'd have felt a bit bad if a good story had been disqualified. On the other hand, there were one or two stories that I wish *could* have been disqualified, because they were too difficult to mark. They were either too good in some aspects or too awful in others, which made the criteria difficult to apply. As a judge you have to deal with that.

[D] Would you say you're a good judge? I'm sure you are, obviously, but how are you better than some of the other judges you've come across?

[G] Well, luckily, I've had feedback on my feedback. In fact, I've had feedback on the feedback on my feedback, if you can get your head around that!

I only had one real complaint from the competitors. I'd suggested that, typical of most British writers, they'd used the word "further" when it should have been "farther". They argued that while I was right to say farther should be used in most instances where distance is involved, and further should be used to make a point, most Brits now use further for both meanings, and it has become acceptable.

Most of the competitors said that while they might not necessarily agree with all of my comments, they were glad I made them. So on that basis I would say I must be a good judge. Though I'm not normally into self-congratulation.

5. How the scoring works

[D] Can you talk about the different criteria and how you scored them?

[G] The categories I looked at were the introduction, characters, inventiveness, voice, the ending, and technical aspects. With minor differences, most competitions use similar scoring.

They were all graded with different weightings:

The opening or introduction was marked out of 10.

The characters were marked out of 15.

Inventiveness out of 20.

Voice out of 30 – that was the highest one.

The ending out of 15.

And the technical aspects out of 10.

[D] That adds up to a total possible score of 100 for each round, and therefore 900 points if they completed all nine rounds. But why is voice weighted so highly? That seems a little strange to me.

[G] Voice includes aspects like plot and the feel of the piece, but I'll talk more about that in a moment.

I wrote notes on what I considered was important for each of these categories. I wasn't given any guidance by the organisers. They said it was up to me as the judge to decide what I thought was important and how to mark it, but it was crucial to me to have a clear idea about these categories.

[D] It would also allow you to maintain consistency throughout the whole judging process.

[G] That's right. There's always an assumption that fiction judges are subjective. There's always going to be *some* subjectivity, but I wanted to try and create reliability – from the scientific use of the word – which means that if I *am* a bit biased in some way, at least the same bias applies all the way through.

[D] Okay, well let's go through each of the categories and perhaps you can talk about what you were looking for.

6. The opening

[G] With the opening it was important that there was a hook in the first paragraph or two. Was that hook a conflict that piqued interest, or a setting intriguingly portrayed that made me want to read on?

Were classic errors avoided? For example, starting with unattributed dialogue, or starting with a dangling participle. These are common errors. Anyone who enters competitions should have read at least one of the many how-to guides and know to avoid these things. It's surprising how many people *do* start a story with a dangling participle. That means a *gerund* – a verb with an "–ing" at the end of it. For example, somebody wrote:

Closing the door, he said, "Hello" and sat down.

Now, it's unlikely that someone would sit and speak *while closing* a door. People sometimes write without thinking about the visual image or exact sequence of events –what's *actually* happening.

[D] That's not a great opening anyway, is it? There's no hook, nothing that immediately grabs you.

[G] It's an awful opening, and the unattributed dialogue isn't a good idea either. If you start off with speech and don't say who said it, then the reader has no idea if this is a man or a woman or a child or a dog speaking. This is the beginning of a new story, so they don't know who the characters are yet. If there's a clue in the next line, it's sometimes forgivable – your mind can backtrack a little – and it could even make it interesting that way. But sometimes you still have no idea who said it, or why.

Still on introductions or openings:

Does it make me smile in appreciation when a strong, active verb is used instead of a weak, passive one? Is somebody walking quickly, for example, or are they running. Walking quickly is a passive verb, whereas running or charging is an interesting active one.

Has a clever phrase set the scene, or introduced a character already? In other words, is there a strong hook right at the beginning?

7. Characters

[G] The next important aspect was character. What some people may not appreciate is that a mark for character in one story might not exactly match the mark for character in another story – even one written by the same person. That's because the mark depends on such things as how the characters relate to the story as a whole.

Are they distinct in their behaviour, voice and appearance? In so many stories you get several characters who are all the same, and their voices are all the same.

Does a character undergo a change in the course of the story? Now, this is a well-known aspect of fiction-writing generally, but it's surprising how many people don't do it.

Is the character interesting? If the character is nice, does the writer go the extra mile to make him or her convincing and worthy of the story?

Does the writer make me feel that I know the characters?

Do all the characters have a role in the story, in that each one moves the plot on?

If the character is a cliché – and some might have to be – is there some quirk or trait to lift them off the page?

It isn't always necessary to describe a character, but if described, is it well done? If not described, is my own image of them consistent throughout the story?

Do the character's habits reinforce the image I formed?

Do I care for that character?

Then there's the Factor X – I just have to have a feel for that one. In other words, the characters have to be just a little bit over the top. Think of TV soaps – even if you hate TV soaps – every character is a little over the top from reality. If they're too far over the top then they're not believable. It's the same with fiction. You've got to make them just that little bit over the top to be interesting, but not so much that they're bizarre.

8. Inventiveness

[G] This is mostly self-explanatory. I look for novelty in all the other categories, as well as in the plot lines.

For example, instead of a linear plot – A happened, then B, then C, then D – is there a B then A then D then C, and so on. This isn't essential, and it would need to be done well to avoid confusion.

If aspects of the story are clichéd, is there a coruscating twist or quirkiness to make it interesting?

Am I going to be surprised?

Am I laughing, shocked, or weeping unexpectedly?

9. Voice

[G] These are some of the aspects of voice that I look for in a story:

Has the writer demonstrated a distinctive wordcraft via a character or set of characters? This is rarely successful in an omniscient point of view.

Is there a sensibility or an attitude that flavours the story?

Has the author avoided unwarranted narrative intrusion? This is a wonderful phrase. Or some people put "authorial" in there too, so it's "authorial unwarranted narrative intrusion".

[D] I just call it "author intrusion".

[G] It can be just that, but sometimes it can be warranted. A little bit of author intrusion can be a fun thing. It's like a TV actor glancing at the camera – just a little knowing wink. If it's unwarranted then it should be cut out. Again, this happens more in novels than in short stories. There's rarely enough time in a short story to do this.

Is the attitude of the story – whether exuberant, miserable, edgy, warm, cold, angry, spooky, and so on – convincing and appropriate?

Does the voice of each character – shown by dialogue and behaviour – correspond with their role? Does it work with the story as a whole?

Is active voice rather than passive voice used? In some cases, passive is appropriate, such as to control pace.

Aspects of the plot can influence the voice of a story. For example, a non-linear plot tends to be more interesting. On the other hand, a linear one might be more appropriate if the other aspects create a complex story.

Is the writing tight, with no pleonasms? Now this is one of my favourite things, pleonasms.

[D] I know! You're always going on about them. But a lot of people won't know what a pleonasm is, so you'd better explain it.

[G] A pleonasm is a word that if removed leaves the sense unchanged. This can include tautologies, though not always.

For example, the words that some writers and editors call "stutter words", like *just*, *still*, *even*, *actually*, *really* and *that*.

If you go through your story and remove all of these, it rarely makes any difference to the sense of the piece, yet it feels tighter.

Sometimes they *are* needed, and you have to make a judgement on that – for example to adjust the pace of a story.

People tend to use pleonasms when they speak in real life. But if your characters speak like that in your story, it will become looser. You can't use speech just as real people use it, otherwise there would be too many "umms" and "ahhs" and too much looseness in there.

Continuing with voice:

Is there good use of show over tell?

Where appropriate, does the writer engage the reader's senses, such as smell, vision (including colours), sound (in addition to dialogue), taste and touch?

If you can, avoid the dreaded nodding. Now, nodding and shrugging are good body language, and quite succinct. Just mentioning somebody shrugging can cut out some dialogue. The problem is, as one editor, Alan Guthrie[1], once said, "Whenever I see a nod, a shrug or a sigh is sure to follow." They are good body language, but overdone, so it's best to avoid them. Use one of them maybe once every thousand words and you might get away with it.

Avoid weak modifiers such as *slightly*, *almost*, and *nearly* – and most adverbs too. The problem with weak modifiers is that after a while the story becomes weak as well, because there isn't enough strength in the narrative.

Is the description just enough to stimulate the reader's imagination and own experience, rather than there being so much that it feels like a list?

Most stories need conflict and resolution. If not, is there intrigue or mystery to engage the reader?

[1] Alan Guthrie is a successful author, agent, and editor of *Hard Luck Stories*.

10. The ending

[G] Has the conflict in the hook been resolved? In some of the stories I read for the Whittaker Prize, there was no real conflict in the hook, and therefore no conflict to resolve for the ending. So they scored low on both the opening and the ending.

Has a twist created a satisfying conclusion?

If there *is* a twist, does the whole story depend on it? This is not usually a good idea.

Does the ending leave the reader with a warm glow? Or annoyed? Does it matter if the reader is annoyed? After all, if you create *any* kind of reaction in a reader, sometimes that's good enough to make them go – on reflection – "Hmm, I liked that!"

Endings don't have to explain *everything*, and they could create more questions than answers.

Have the main characters undergone a change, revealed in the latter part of the piece?

[D] Could someone have a bad opening or a bad ending but still make up enough points to win – perhaps by being outstandingly original or having great characters?

[G] It *is* possible. In the Whittaker Prize, the opening and the ending between them make up 30 marks out of the possible 100. The problem is that if the story has a very low score for the opening, it usually means there's no conflict or hook. If that's the case then there can be no resolution at the end – so what's the plot about? What's happening in the middle? Nevertheless, it would be possible to have a medium-scoring story if it only had a middle.

[D] I invited members of the ideas4writers Facebook group to send in questions they wanted us to discuss. One of the things they particularly wanted to know about was twist endings. Is there anything else you can say about them?

[G] There are a few competitions and anthologies where the whole point of them is to have a twist at the end. But most magazine anthologies and competitions don't like it *if* the whole story depends on that twist. In other words, if it comes out of the blue.

The worst is a *Deus ex machina*, where a problem is suddenly resolved with no prior clues. For example, a previously undisclosed escape pod in an exploding spaceship. These usually irritate the reader – especially if it ends up with the whole thing being a dream.

[D] That's awful, isn't it. You really mustn't do that. Again, it just screams "amateur", and you have no chance of winning. Or of ever getting it published.

[G] Here's a good example. It's quite a well-known one. It went around the internet many years ago, so it may be old to you or it may be new to you, but the twist at the end is quite a nice one:

Dear Mum and Dad,

I do hope you will be understanding in what I have done. Remember that I love you both very much.

I have left with Patrick. You would like him if you knew him. In fact, you might, since he was in the year above you at school.

I love him very much and he has promised to marry me when his second divorce comes through.

I have dropped out of university to move to Patrick's city. We are coping surprisingly well in the inner-city squat Patrick has found for us.

We do not have much money until Patrick gets a job, but I'm going to sell my antique doll collection and the computer to buy things for the baby when it comes in a few weeks' time.

Love Angie

P.S. None of the above is true. I just wanted you to get things into perspective for when my exam results come through.

So that's quite a nice one – more of a joke than a story.

[D] I've definitely heard it before. It's been around for years.

[G] It has, but it's surprising how many people haven't heard it. It's an example of a twist at the end that can be quite amusing. But it's dangerous to use them in short stories, especially in competitions.

[D] Do you like twist endings?

[G] I do like twist endings, and I have written several. But it's important that the twist is something like a fun add-on, or something that I didn't expect to happen, rather than something that changes the whole story.

I certainly don't like it if it turns out that somebody totally different was telling the story, rather than the person we've been led to believe.

12. Dialogue

[G] One of the judging criteria for many competitions is dialogue. There have been some interesting changes in dialogue in recent years, particularly with dialogue tags or speech tags. These are the things that go at the beginning or end of a speech and tell the reader who has just spoken. For example: "It's a nice day," said John.

Now, the word "said" – according to almost all the how-to books – is said to be invisible. So you can use *said* rather than words like *blurted*, *yelled* or *said quietly*. If you use too many different types of dialogue tag, the reader allegedly becomes tired of them, or doesn't like them. So the word *said* was supposed to be the one you always used.

Not only that, but the tag was supposed to come *after* the name of the character. So instead of saying *said John* it should be *John said*. It's logical in a way, because the readers know more quickly who is speaking.

However, dialogue tags have changed, and they're now being dropped. In other words, you're phrasing the whole paragraph so that you can tell who's speaking from the context alone. So you don't need any dialogue tags at all.

The first author who I noticed had done this in a successful way was A. L. Kennedy. When I was reading her collection of short stories *Now That You're Back*, I was two-thirds of the way through the book before I realised that she'd used no dialogue tags at all. She's an absolute ace at doing that.

However, not everyone is such an expert. In *The Other Boleyn Girl*, for example, Philippa Roberts tried to remove many of the dialogue tags. But I sometimes found myself having to turn back two or three pages to work out who was saying what to whom. So it didn't work in that case.

I think you need a mixture of both, especially for beginning writers. You do need to have some *saids*. And not just *saids* – if someone is yelling, there's nothing wrong with saying *yelling*. If a character is whispering, you can say so.

For a good dialogue mark in a competition, you could try doing other things. Oblique dialogue is a good technique. This is where two people are having a conversation, but one of them isn't listening. It's as if they're responding to different questions. You shouldn't have too many pages of oblique dialogue, but it's quite fun to do, and it makes the reader feel as though it's more realistic.

Related to dialogue is action and reaction to the speaker by other characters.

Try not to have pages of dialogue with no physical action of any sort.

[D] One other point on speech tags is that you need to watch out for things like *he smiled* or *he grinned*. For example, "Ah, you're back at last," John smiled. These aren't actually speech tags, they're facial expressions.

[G] Yes, that's true – and especially *laughed*. You often get people saying, "John, do you want a cup of tea?" she laughed. Now, laughing is not a speech verb. And as you say, nor is smiling.

Even if you think it's appropriate, and you build up an argumentative case for an editor to show that your speech tag could be logical, it's still an "amateur alert" flag. So avoid it!

[D] Would you suggest *John said with a laugh*, or *he said, smiling* or something like that?

[G] Yes. Or make it a separate sentence: "Ah, you're back at last." John smiled. Or have it obvious in the context, which would be smarter and tighter.

[D] How much dialogue should you have in your story?

[G] One of the best practitioners of short stories is Della Galton. She's been writing them for a long time, and she believes that about thirty percent of the text in a short story should be dialogue. It's a rough figure, and these are for her type of stories, which are generally aimed at the women's magazine market.

I find that if short stories have almost no dialogue, they're hard work to read, because the dialogue can often be part of the "show" rather than the "tell". It can help the readers to engage more with the characters if they're inside their heads while they're speaking.

[D] Would a lot of dialogue turn you off?

[G] Yes, if there's too much. If there's much more, or much less, than thirty percent dialogue, then it tends to be not such a well-balanced story.

I've written, as an experiment, stories which are *all* dialogue, so it's like a playscript. It *can* work – it all depends on the circumstances. A flash story – one that's round about 1,000 words or less – is best suited to an all-dialogue story. For a short story, probably a third to a half of it should be dialogue.

13. Technical aspects

[G] Finally, we come to the technical bits. Not all competitions have a technical aspect to them. It's a bit like the GCSE and A-Level examinations in Britain, which still have a SPAG mark – a **SP**elling **A**nd **G**rammar mark – which is five percent of the total. In short story competitions, the SPAG mark can also include Americanisms or British English.

The technical aspects are generally given in the competition guidelines, which all entrants should adhere to. For example:

Has the writer exceeded the maximum number of words?

Is the submission formatted correctly?

There was a bit of formatting involved in the guidelines for the Whittaker competition: it needed to be double-spaced, and the font had to be Times New Roman and 12pt. To be honest, it only takes a few seconds to change that in Microsoft Word, so it didn't bother me too much, and I didn't mark anybody down for formatting errors.

[D] So all of the entries were sent in by email?

[G] Yes, though they didn't have to be in Word format, they could be RTF (Rich Text Format). But they had to be emailed, not printed.

Competitors might have lost one of their ten technical marks if they had a few typos. But if there were a lot of them, and they were annoying, they would lose more. Or if there were plot or character errors. For example, if a Jane became a Janet. Or if there was a change of physical appearance without any good reason for it. Or if a character killed on page 1 became alive again on page 3, yet it wasn't a horror or a fantasy story.

So those were the main judging criteria. They weren't hard and fast, and sometimes an outstanding story could flag a lot of those points and still win.

[D] Would you accept a story if someone submitted it and then sent in a page of corrections afterwards?

[G] In most competitions there is a strict deadline, but if a contestant sent their story in early, and then decided they'd bungled and wanted to send in corrections, it wasn't too much of a problem from the organisers' point of view. They said, "Look, we know you've already read and marked this story, but we're asking you to read and mark it again." I always did.

[D] Would you prefer people to send in the entire story again, or just the corrections?

[G] The entire story again. I don't want to have to count down the page to find line 24 and insert a "but".

15. Choosing the winner

[D] How would you choose between two stories with identical scores?

[G] I gave a couple of people identical scores, so there were two winners for that particular round. I didn't have a problem with that. I wasn't sure how the organisers would cope. I suppose I could have gone through both stories and nit-picked and found one winner. Like life, it just happens. I try to be as objective as I can with the criteria, and that's what happens sometimes. So they got the same score.

In the 2009 competition, Catherine Edmonds had the higher score by several points in the end. With 900 points on offer altogether, the chances of two people having exactly the same number of points after all nine rounds isn't likely. Though I think there were one or two people with equal scores lower down the list.

[D] And how about if you were judging the more common type of contest where people only submit one story each? What would happen then if the top two entries were equally matched?

[G] If I had to make a choice then I *would* be able to – but reluctantly.

Generally speaking, for anyone to get into the top five in the Whittaker Prize, they have to be outstanding writers. Incidentally, *all* of the authors were good. It's a shame because I know that one or two writers in that competition have now given up writing because they didn't get into the top three, or they were only middling in the rounds and they were hoping to do much better. Of course, I didn't know who they were until afterwards. To my chagrin, I discovered that one or two of them said, "Oh, that's it then" – and they're not going to write any more.

All of the writers from that competition had been critiquing each other and working hard at their craft, and so they were *all* good.

It would have been tough to separate them, but I could have done it if I'd been made to.

[D] Have you ever given anyone a perfect score?

[G] No. I'm afraid I was a tough marker as a school teacher. In fact, the competitors wouldn't have expected me to give a perfect score. I only awarded perfect scores for the technical aspects. In other words, if they'd got all of their spelling and grammar absolutely correct – I wouldn't have dropped any marks for misplaced commas. Generally, their spelling and grammar and the other technical criteria were absolutely spot-on, so I awarded most stories the full ten points for that category.

As for the other marks, there's *always* something that could be improved upon – just as there is in my own work. So none of the other criteria achieved perfect scores. A high score would be in the region of 80 to 85 out of 100.

[D] What would the ideal winning entry look like?

[G] It had to be from the left field, hitting me in the stomach partway through. A winning story is one which is well written and has a transcendental quality, but somewhere around two-thirds to three-quarters of the way through, something happens that knocks me sideways.

One of the winning entries for one of the rounds was like that, where it turned out that one of the characters – side-lined throughout the story until that point – was the writer himself. It's dangerous to do this, and generally a real no-no to have the author as the narrator. In this case it was a surprise, and superbly done. There was no way that that story couldn't win that round.

[D] What can you do to make your story stand out from all the other entries? Is it simply a case of knowing what the criteria are and aiming to get the highest score for each of them?

[G] To a certain extent it is. But it also has to have originality, some lateral thinking – and this buzz that comes out of the left field, as the Americans have it.

If, as in the Whittaker competition, you're given prompts, and let's say there's a dog in the prompt, you know that a lot of people are going to be writing with that theme. Yours has got to stand out. It's got to have some sort of original idea to have a chance of winning.

16. The longlist and the shortlist

[D] Several members of the ideas4writers Facebook group wanted to know the difference between a longlist and a shortlist.

[G] We didn't have a longlist or a shortlist at the Whittaker Prize, but many other competitions do – the Bridport Prize and other prestigious prizes, and the Man Booker Prize, of course, for novels.

For competitions where there are many entries, obviously you have to have some weeding out. I think *Richard & Judy* (the former British TV show) had 10,000 entries in their competition. In cases like that, you'll get people who aren't necessarily editors looking at the entries as they come in, looking for ways to eliminate them. In other words, they're removing all the ones that haven't met the criteria. At the end of that, you get a list of several hundred people who *did* match all the submission guidelines, so their stories can be read seriously.

[D] The entries on the longlist are those that have made it through the preliminary rounds of judging, or have scored higher than a certain cut-off point. This is the longlist that goes through to the *serious* judging stage. Those that survive *that* process will make it onto the shortlist. If there are celebrity judges, this is generally where they get involved. They'll usually only read the stories on the shortlist, once all the others have been eliminated.

17. Finding competitions to enter

[D] If you're looking for suitable competitions to enter, how would you go about finding them?

[G] The best way is to simply type "writing competitions" into Google. You'll find thousands of them.

The writing magazines – *Writers' Forum*[1], *Writing Magazine*[2], *Writer's Digest*[3] and so on – tend to run a news item when there's a competition coming up. And the editors of these magazines will also have vetted them to make sure they're legitimate competitions.

[1] www.writers-forum.com

[2] www.writers-online.co.uk

[3] www.writersdigest.com

18. Avoiding scams

[G] You do need to check that any competitions you plan on entering are being run by reputable organisations. There are a few scammy ones out there that just want your entry fee or contact details, or they're grabbing free material to publish in a book or anthology, and you'll never see a penny for it.

There are some simple checks you can do:

- Have you heard of them?

- Do you trust them?

- Do they look legitimate?

- Have they run a competition before?

- Have they published a list of previous winners on their website?

- Have you heard of any of the previous winners?

- Are there any photos of previous winners receiving their prizes?

- Do they have a long-established website or has it just appeared recently?

- Are there lots of pages and sections on their website or is it just a single page advertising their competition?

- Are the rules or guidelines clear and complete and spelt correctly, and are you happy with them?

- Who will judge the competition? Who is sponsoring it? Have you heard of them?

- Do you understand what the prize is, and what rights they will have to publish the winning entries?

- Is the competition mentioned elsewhere when you search for it? For example, in the editorial sections or competition pages of newspapers, magazines and websites you know and trust. It should be more than just an advert.

If any of these things trigger your alarm bells, skip that competition and move on to the next one. There's no shortage of genuine ones.

19. How many competitions should you enter?

[D] How many competitions per year do you recommend people enter?

[G] Ah, that's an interesting one – how much time do you have? I think half a dozen at a time is reasonable. I know of one person who has stories in three hundred competitions at any one time. I didn't know there *were* that many competitions open at any one time. I checked, and found several writers that maintain online lists of current competitions, and some of them *do* list three hundred or more. A quick search for competition listings on Google will produce thousands of them. But you'd need to have a lot of time on your hands to get that number of stories out there.

20. Multiple submissions

[G] Of course, this person doesn't write three hundred *new* stories for each of those different competitions. She's double entering – or *more* than double entering – sending the same story to several competitions at once. That's not entirely within the spirit of things.

[D] That's rather risky too, isn't it?

[G] Yes, because if the same story wins two different competitions she'll be in trouble – not least because of the competition rules about copyright.

21. Transcending quality

[D] How do you think a *winning* short story differs from a *good* short story?

[G] This will be different for each judge, and for each competition. They all have different criteria.

For example, Jon Pinnock is a good writer of short stories, but I gave him a middling mark for one of his entries* in the 2009 Whittaker Prize. However, within two weeks he won a prize in another competition with that same story, because their criteria were quite different. At least, that's the reason I like to think why he won that one and not the Whittaker!

But there's also this *Factor X* that I mentioned earlier. Each writer needs to include something different in a story that boosts it above all the rest. The writer and agent Noah Lukeman talks about a *transcending quality* to a story – it has to have something that transcends it above all the rest. It usually has something to do with imagery. In other words, there are literary phrases that lift it above what people normally write.

Again, one writer that I think has this quality is A. L. Kennedy. Her short stories have a transcendental quality that would win competitions.

For instance, when talking about the sky, most people might talk about clouds scurrying across it, but she writes: *Something impatient about the sky*. Now that to me is a literary phrase. It's succinct, it's tight, it shows you that here you have a literary writer.

For another character, who was in a state of shock, she wrote: *I have temporarily forgotten how to inhale*. A. L. Kennedy has a book of short stories called *Now That You're Back*. Thirteen short stories, each of them brilliant, but especially the title story which is at the back of the book. Some of her lateral thinking becomes lateral writing in such phrases as:

The church has survived by becoming another stone among stones and setting its congregation safe underground.

Phil started another sentence ... then sighed it away again.

The birds had a funny, short way of whistling, as if they were worried over something.

And in describing scenery with few hills:

The landscape had calmed down a little.

You will have your own favourites from other writers like Julian Barnes, China Miéville and other people who are known to be contemporary literary writers. These are the sort of writers that have the Factor X.

> * You can read Jon Pinnock's story, *Return to Cairo*, at the end of this book, along with his scores for each category and the judge's comments.

22. What makes a winning writer?

[D] Do you think there's such a thing as a *typical* competition winner? By which I mean a type of person rather than a story.

[G] Yes, it does tend to be the case that literary writers who have won one competition then go on to win more, or become highly placed. There's a group of them on the internet – all good souls, and they're solid gold writers.

I thought I'd be able to identify their individual styles. So I was worried when I started judging the Whittaker competition because I knew several of them, even though their work was coming to me anonymously.

For example, I know one of them is an artist, so you get a lot of descriptions of colours in terms of paint pigments: burnt sienna and so on. Another is a musician, so he tends to work musical terms into his stories. But I was wrong almost every time when the writers' names were revealed after each round. They all have excellent literary style. They know each other and their strong points, and they tend to mimic each other to a certain extent in competitions. Partly out of devilment and fun, but also because they know they're good writers and they relish playing with each other's specialities. So, yes, you do tend to get the same writers in the top five or so.

[D] Do you think *anyone* can write winning short stories? Can you learn how to do it? Or do you have to be born a writer?

[G] That's an interesting question. Anyone can write a short story, but I think it might be foolish or naïve to think that anyone can write a *winning* short story. Depending on the competition, of course, and how many entries there are. Only a privileged few have the level of lateral thinking that's required to pull off a winning story. Having said that, you can learn to be a lateral thinker. So, if you can learn to be a lateral thinker, maybe you can learn to be a lateral writer!

23. The most popular genres

[D] Is any particular genre of short story more popular, more in demand, or better paying than the others?

[G] The most popular, and the most in-demand, and the best paid stories are the ones for women's magazines. There's no doubt about that.

Following that, probably the science fiction magazines, though sadly there are only one or two in Britain, and the rest are American. As recession strikes both countries, the magazines tend to publish only well-known writers because they sell more copies. So the lesser-known writers have more of a struggle to get into those magazines.

[D] And is there a genre that tends to do better in competitions?

[G] I would say the literary genre fares better in competitions than any other. By literary I mean those that don't fall easily into any other genre. If they do fall into another genre, they still need to be *literally* well written to stand a good chance.

24. Stories that don't work

[D] In your experience, what's the main reason why some stories don't succeed?

[G] One of the main ones, incredibly, is that they're illegible. Of course, they've been written on a computer, so they *shouldn't* be illegible. But some people write right up to the deadline, and they don't leave themselves enough time to create a draft, then go through it and edit and proofread it. So they get their words mixed up. They ought to read it aloud to themselves, and then the errors would leap out.

Sometimes they use loose language or they're clichéd to bits. Look at the characters in TV soaps, because they're the sort of characters that are over the top but not too unbelievable on the whole. They would work well in short stories – or any fiction. But one of the things that characters in TV soaps do is talk in clichés all the time. It's almost as if the dialogue is one long cliché. You mustn't do that in a short story – and especially not for a competition – because although people *do* talk in clichés, you need something better in your writing.

Above all, you mustn't let the story feel pedestrian, or it won't make it into the top ten.

25. Mistakes and reasons for disqualification

[D] What are the main reasons why stories get disqualified from competitions?

[G] The main reasons are that they're too long and go over the prescribed word count limit, or they're wrongly formatted, or they're aiming at the wrong target.

[D] And what are the main mistakes people make?

[G] The main mistakes are:

- They haven't read the guidelines.

- They've probably used authorial intrusion, as we discussed earlier.

- They've not read their story out loud, and they haven't done their rewriting.

- They've messed up their pronouns. That's quite a common fault, in that they'll mention a *his* or *they*, for which there is a strict pronoun rule. A pronoun refers to the main prior subject, but the way they've written it, it often doesn't.

- Many stories don't have a conflict of any sort, so there's no hook, and no story resolution.

[D] What would you say is the biggest mistake beginners make with their writing?

[G] Being too loose, there's no doubt about that. New writers, generally speaking, haven't read the how-to books or been on any of the forums yet, so they tend to write far too loosely. In other words, they're using words like *just* and *even* and *actually*, and overusing the word *that*.

I used to make *that* mistake. When I first sent off a novel to be critiqued, it came back saying "Expunge your thats!" So I did, and my novel was nearly 2,000 words shorter – and all the better for it. Of course, you don't get rid of every *that* – some of them are necessary. That's the thing: you go through and find words you don't need.

Another mistake is word and phrase echoes. People tend to write the same thing again and again. They might not see it – it's invisible to them – but a critiquer will look at it and say, "Hey, did you realise you used that same word in the previous sentence?"

A new writer tends to start at the beginning and go to the end. They like to set the scene. But if you're not careful it's like talking to your grandmother. You know, when you say, "Gosh, Gran, you've hurt your leg. How did that happen?" and you're expecting her to say, "I tripped over my bicycle", but instead she says, "Well, when I got up this morning I couldn't find the tea bags, so I needed to go to the Spar shop…" You don't need all that, do you? But that's what inexperienced writers do. One of the best pieces of advice you can give a writer is to start a scene late and finish it early.

By doing these things, you'll find that your writing tightens itself up, and you'll tend to think more about *how* you're writing it, so the reader will feel it's exciting.

26. Should you research the judges?

[D] Let's switch roles for a moment and consider the situation where you're entering a competition rather than judging it.

If you knew in advance who the judges were, would you do some research on them to find out about their likes and dislikes and so on?

[G] It would make sense to do that. For example, I know one of the regular winners and runners-up of competitions in the annual Winchester Writers' Festival[1], and she goes to a lot of trouble to find out who the judges are going to be for the various categories. Then she researches what they've written and published, and what their likes and dislikes are. She then writes according to that – and sometimes wins.

However, there are dangers in researching them. In the 2009 Whittaker competition, several competitors knew that I write science fiction. (I write thrillers and humour stories too.) Sadly, the competitors who thought they'd give me a treat and write a science fiction story *surely* must have known that I've read thousands of them, because I was also the co-editor of *Escape Velocity* magazine. We had hundreds of submissions every month, many of which, for example, were on alien abductions. Now, that's a good story, alien abductions, but to make yours stand out from all the others it would have to be *fantastic* – in every sense of the word.

Unless you really know the judge's genre well, it's probably best to avoid it, otherwise you're going to make that sort of "amateur feel" mistake.

Most judges, although they may have a leaning towards one genre or another, enjoy reading outside that genre too. It's a refreshing change for them.

[D] All the different genres have their own sets of rules, conventions and tropes that need to be followed. If you're writing outside your normal genre, you might not know what they are. You could easily come across as an amateur even if you're a brilliant writer in your own genre.

The same sort of thing happened to me when I was judging my own competitions. Several people researched me, the area where I live, my interests, and so on, and they wrote stories about that, or made it a major component of their stories. Some of the stories even featured a main character called Dave, which is making it rather obvious!

Some were set in the area where I live – although they clearly didn't know the area terribly well. And some wrote stories about my interests – which are pretty wide-ranging, from writing and publishing, marketing, computer programming, science and technology, art and electronic music, to ghost hunting and the paranormal, to name but a few. But I've been doing those things, and studying them quite intensely, for years – decades, in fact – and they were writing about subjects that were new to them. So their stories were full of basic factual inaccuracies, clichés, false assumptions, and beginner-level humour. I found them quite excruciating and embarrassing to read, and I rejected them

on those grounds alone, regardless of how good they might have been otherwise.

[G] Here's another example from the Whittaker Prize of pandering to the judge. The competitors know I have a … not a fetish exactly, but I'm keen on sensory show in my writing, and I like to see it in others. Once they discover this, some authors who don't normally write about colours and sense of smell and sounds other than dialogue, start throwing them in everywhere. So you'd get a sentence with five different colours.

One of the things that many beginning writers don't appreciate when they're using smells is that your olfactory senses get confused if you're smelling more than one or two smells at one time. It ends up being "brown", if you know what I mean. So when a character goes into a room, you find their noses being assaulted by different spices. There's rose scent in one corner, and a smelly dog scratching itself in another, and somebody's walking past wearing gardenia perfume, and… No! No! This is overkill! You have to be careful about overdoing sensory show.

[1] http://writersfestival.co.uk

27. Clichés, over-used plots, and other frequent mistakes

[D] Let's talk about clichés now. You've brought along a list of things we should all avoid.

[G] Yes. Some kind publishers decided to cut down on the time they spent reading submissions by publishing a list of the story premises they didn't want to see any more. Now, this doesn't mean these stories are bad. It just means they see an awful lot of them, so yours would have to be outstanding in order to get a look in.

This list is from *Strange Horizons*[1], an online speculative fiction magazine. They have several lists of what fiction *not* to send them. They're mostly about horror and science fiction, but the advice also applies to romance, crime, and other genres.

These are the plot ideas they suggest you avoid[2]:

1. Person is (metaphorically) at point A, wants to be at point B. Looks at point B, says "I want to be at point B". Walks to point B, encountering no meaningful obstacles or difficulties.

    This is a linear plot. Try to avoid stories of that form.

2. A creative person is having trouble creating. Publishers and judges receive many stories where:

    -   a writer has writer's block

    -   a painter can't seem to paint anything good

    -   a sculptor can't seem to sculpt

    -   the creative person's work is reviled by critics, who don't understand how brilliant it is

- the creative person meets a muse – either one of the nine classical muses, or a more individual one – and interacts with them, usually by keeping them captive

Now, these things happen to all of us writers – well, maybe not that last one so much – but you have to try and resist the temptation to write about them as part of a competition.

3. A visitor to an alien planet ignores information about the local rules, inadvertently violates them, and is punished.

   This story doesn't have to be about aliens in the extraterrestrial sense: the interloper could have arrived on an unsophisticated island on Earth, and so on.

4. A protagonist is a bad person. We don't object to this in a story, we just object to it being the main point of the plot.

   - The bad person is told they'll get the reward they *deserve* – which, of course, ends up being something bad.

   - Terrorists discover that horrible things happen to them in their afterlife, or they get their comeuppance in other ways.

     For several years, Osama bin Laden was the main character in many of these stories.

   - A protagonist is portrayed as awful, but that portrayal is merely a set-up for the ending, in which they see the error of their ways and are redeemed.

There are far too many of these stories.

5. A place is described, but there's no plot or characters.

   I was surprised, in the Whittaker competition, that I received some stories with no characters at all. So, therefore, I was unable to award any points for the characterisation category. It's important to always examine the competition's guidelines and make sure you include all the elements of the criteria.

6. A "surprise" twist ending occurs.

   We like endings that we don't expect, as long as they derive naturally from the character action. We've seen a lot of twist endings and we find most of them to be pretty predictable. The *Strange Horizons* website has a long list of twists that keep appearing time after time, but you should be careful to avoid *any* kind of predictable twist, even if it isn't on the list. Here are a few examples of what to avoid:

   - The characters are described as if they're humans, but in the end it turns out they're not. Or characters are described as vermin or pests or monsters, but in the end it turns out they're humans.

   - The author conceals some essential piece of information from the reader that would be obvious if the reader were present at the scene. This information is suddenly revealed at the end of the story. This *can* be done well, but it rarely is.

- A person is floating in a formless void, and in the end ... they're born.

- A person uses time travel to achieve a particular result, but in the end something unexpected happens that thwarts their plan.

- The main point of the story is for the author to metaphorically tell the reader, "Ha, ha, I tricked you! You thought one thing was going on, but it was something else! You sure are dumb!" Try to avoid stories like that.

7. A scientist uses himself (or herself) as the test subject.

8. An evil, unethical doctor performs medical experiments on an unsuspecting patient.

9. Office life turns out to be soul-deadening – literally or metaphorically.

10. In the future, criminals are punished much more harshly than they are today. Usually by the punishment fitting the crime exactly.

11. A white protagonist is given wise and mystical advice by a holy, simple, native person.

12. An alien observes and comments on the peculiar habits of humans, for allegedly comic effect.

- The alien is fluent in English and familiar with various English idioms, but is completely unfamiliar with human biology, or with such concepts as sex or violence, or with certain extremely common English words.

- Or the alien takes everything literally.

13. Person A tells a story to Person B (or to a room full of people) about Person C. In the end, it turns out that:

    - Person B *is* Person C

    - Person A *is* Person C (or has the same goals)

14. Finally, people whose politics are different from the author's are shown to be stupid, insane, or evil – usually through satire, sarcasm, stereotyping, and wild exaggeration.

    - For example, in the future, the USA or the world is ruled by politically correct liberals, leading to awful things.

    - Or in the future, the USA or the world is ruled by fascist conservatives, leading to awful things.

So those are the sort of plot themes you should try to avoid. One of the reasons why they have become so common is that they were recommended as a writing formula many years ago by an American science fiction agent called Scott Meredith. It seemed to work well, and a lot of people liked those sort of stories in the 1950s and 1960s, but there are just too many of them now.

[1] http://strangehorizons.com

[2] You can find the full list of stories to avoid here: http://strangehorizons.com/submit/fiction-submission-guidelines/stories-weve-seen-too-often/

28. Professional writers and competitions

[D] Do professional writers enter short story competitions, or is it something they stop doing once they become well known or start making money?

[G] Most of them don't have the time. I know several full-time novelists who may have started off writing short stories, and occasionally still write shorts now, but not for competitions. Their calendars are extraordinarily full. They're filled up by both their agents and by their publishers for readings, signings, deadlines, and so on.

The only exception is that because there are so many short story competitions available for science fiction, authors who write in that genre may be directed by their agents to enter those competitions because it improves the sales of their novels.

29. Writing for publication versus writing for competitions

[D] How do you think a short story written for a competition differs from one written for publication – in a magazine for example?

[G] This varies with the magazine. Some magazine stories are more loose. The dialogue is allowed to have more cliché – or even *encouraged* to contain cliché. And there are different targets: the magazines tend to be targeted towards specific genres or readers. Stories in women's magazines tend to be quite different from competition entry stories.

Having said that, they're *all* getting tougher. If you read some of the good stories in some of the women's magazines these days, as well as the science fiction ones and others, you'll find that the writing is getting tighter all the time.

30. Copyright and other rights

[D] Where do writers stand on copyright, and other rights, if their story wins or is shortlisted?

[G] You have to be careful with this. You must read all the small print for every competition you enter.

A good competition, with ethical administration, will let you keep the copyright to your story but allow them first-time rights to publish it in an anthology or on their website. This particularly applies if you win it, or if you're in, say, the first three.

There are competitions where, simply by entering them, you give away your copyright and all rights to your story in perpetuity. The organisers can then publish it or reuse it in any sort of format they like, including print, electronic formats, anthologies, audio, TV, films, computer games, or anything else. You can't cancel it, and you won't ever get paid – you've given it away. It's important to scrutinise the guidelines closely.

You cannot copyright an idea or a title, though, so be careful about that. Whenever you publish a story, whether on your own website, or on a forum, or enter it into a competition, other people could use your ideas. That's not the same as using your story. They would have to be careful that they didn't copy it word-for-word or person-for-person, because that would be plagiarism, which is illegal.

[D] So the organisers could publish your story in an anthology and make money from it, while you, the writer, don't receive a penny.

[G] They could certainly do that if they choose to, and if they say in their guidelines that they have the right to do so. But many new writers are pleased that they've done well in a competition. They're usually so chuffed that they're going to be published in an anthology – even if it's one they have to pay for – that they'll happily go along with it.

However, in five or ten years' time you might decide you want to include that story in a different anthology. If the organisation that ran the competition grabbed all the rights in perpetuity, they now own that story. It's not yours any more, and you no longer have any right to use it.

If they only took the first-time rights to publish it, then it's still yours and you *can* reuse it. It's important to check what rights to the story you have and what rights the competition organisers have.

If you think you might want to reuse or sell the story in the future, make sure the competition guidelines make it clear that they'll only take *first-time rights*. If they want *all rights*, then you shouldn't enter that story. Submit one you never intend reusing, or don't enter that competition at all.

31. Rewriting and resubmitting

[D] If your story doesn't win, would you submit it for another competition, or try to get it published? Or would you recommend reworking it first?

[G] I would recommend rewriting it first, especially if it has come from a competition that gave feedback.

Of course, you may not agree with the feedback. Just because I had to write critiques for the Whittaker and FicFun competitions doesn't mean they all agreed with what I said. It was still only one person's subjective opinion.

But yes, definitely submit it somewhere else, whether for a another competition or for publication. One piece of advice that appears in all of the how-to books is to write-write-write and submit-submit-submit.

Don't be disheartened if one person didn't like your story enough for it to win a competition. If the winners hadn't entered that particular competition, or maybe if there had been a different judge, yours might have been the one that won.

[D] You wouldn't want to be in the position, though, where you've just got one set of stories that you think are "good enough" and you keep sending them to the same competitions over and over again, year after year.

[G] Well, some people *do* do that!

32. Transitioning from runner-up to winner

[D] How can we help someone who's a perennial runner-up, or always comes second and never quite manages to win? This is another question from a member of the ideas4writers Facebook group.

[G] I was in that situation with my novel *Exit, Pursued by a Bee*, which was entered into a readers' poll for new novels. My book came second out of 160 entries in the science fiction novel category. On the last day, it was in first place for several hours. Then the winning book, *Slow Train to Arcturus* by Eric Flint and Dave Freer, rallied enough readers and friends to vote mine out of the top spot. That's annoying! I got a "Top Ten Finalist" badge to put on my website, and acquired the kudos of being good enough to be second.

But how to get to that number one spot ... well, it's just luck. If the person who was number one hadn't entered then *you* would have been number one. It's best not to be disheartened. Just keep plugging away and resubmitting.

33. Which competitions make the best targets?

[D] Do you think it's better to target smaller competitions first, or go for the bigger ones with bigger prizes and more kudos?

[G] Definitely the smaller ones first. The larger ones can be quite expensive to enter, they often don't give any feedback, and you might not even know whether your entry has been received. Of course, if your story is outstanding and you're certain you have a good chance of being shortlisted, then enter it. But if you're just starting out, then entering a smaller competition that gives feedback should be your priority.

[D] As a writer, do you think it's better to target open competitions or themed ones? And by that, I mean a competition where you can write absolutely anything, versus one where the organisers dictate the genre, subject or first line, or give you some sort of prompt.

[G] It all depends. I prefer open competitions, but if you only write in one particular genre, then look for a competition that has that as its theme. As a writer, I hate being given a first line or a prompt. I feel it stifles my creativity. On the other hand, many writers find such prompts and first lines a challenge and a stimulus to their creativity. We are all different.

[D] But isn't it the case that themed competitions receive fewer entries, so you therefore stand a better chance of winning?

[G] They *do* have fewer entries. I know of several that have had to be cancelled because of a lack of entries. It's surprising how few entries there are for some of them.

[D] So if you find one you can enter, then enter it. You might stand a better chance than you think!

As a judge, do you prefer open themes, or set themes, or set first lines, or do you have no preference?

[G] I much prefer an open theme. I get bored pretty quickly, so to have a themed competition, and to have to read hundreds of horse-riding horror stories, for example, would drive me mad. Having an open theme where I can assess a mixture of science fiction and horror and thrillers and romance and so on is much more interesting.

34. Increasing your chances of success

[D] What else can writers do to increase their chances of success?

[G] Make sure your writing is excellent, and that you have an original idea if possible – or at least an original take on an idea. Your writing also needs to be tight. Ideally, you'll have had it critiqued, or at the very least you'll have read it out loud to yourself.

And you'll have done all the usual things, such as reading the rules, keeping within the word count limit, and formatting it correctly.

If you enter a competition that has a high entry fee, that'll weed out a lot of people.

But the trouble is you're looking to *win* a competition, and the other potential winners will have done all of those things too. So in the end, it's still going to be down to luck that your story is regarded by the judges as being better than everyone else's.

It would be a good idea to find out who won the competition last year and the year before, and see what sort of style they had, and what sort of things please the judges. Check who the judges are. Look at the sort of things they like to read about and the style they like to follow. Good luck!

[D] As a male writer, do you generally prefer to read works by male authors? And does that influence your judging?

[G] No, it doesn't. There are excellent writers of both genders. I find that female writers describe things more than male writers do, especially clothing and jewellery. That's not a negative or a positive thing to say; I enjoy the writings of both genders.

[D] And does the gender of the main character matter to you?

[G] No. Not at all.

36. Humour

[D] Is there a place for humour in short story competitions?

[G] Well, *I'm* a humorist, in the sense that almost everything I write has humour in it – even when I don't want there to be. I think ironic humour is the best sort to colour a short story. What you don't want – and what I've had to expunge from my own writing – are quips. Having too many quips and jokes in a story is a sign of amateur writing.

The occasional joke a particular character tells might be part of his characterisation: he's a joker, and he jokes to make light of a difficult situation. Many people use humour to alleviate their pain, so that's okay.

But humour may be inappropriate in some types of horror story, or certain types of poignant relationship stories. There's usually a place for humour in most genres: it helps lighten moods, creates atmosphere, adjusts pace, and colours in characters.

[D] What sort of humour do *you* like?

[G] Neil Marr, who used to run BeWrite Books, told me about this funny incident:

> Despite a reputation for seriousness, Graham Greene, who wrote *The Third Man* and *Our Man in Havana*, enjoyed parody, even of himself. In 1949, when *The New Statesman* held a contest for parodies of Greene's writing style, he submitted an entry under the *nom de plume* N. Wilkinson. He came second – in a competition for his own writing style! The first prize was awarded to his younger brother, Hugh.

I think that's hilarious!

37. Plot-driven stories versus character-driven stories

[D] Do you prefer a fast-moving story or something more character-driven?

[G] It depends on my mood. I like fast-moving stories, but the problem with them is that they're often *too* highly paced, so there's little time for characters to develop or for other aspects of the story to form. If I had to make a choice, it would be a character-driven story.

38. Style

[D] Do you prefer stories written in a similar style to your own?

[G] No, absolutely not. For a long time, I've avoided reading stories written in my *genre*, let alone my style. I've been told that my thriller style is similar to that of Mark Billingham, so I've deliberately not read any of his work. I don't want to accidentally copy other writers.

I prefer to read stories that are written quite differently from mine.

On the other hand, I admire the lateral thinking of writers such as Julian Barnes and A. L. Kennedy, and I can't help being influenced by their style.

39. Taboo subjects

[D] What subjects are taboo in short story competitions?

[G] It all depends on the competition. I don't think there was anything that was stipulated to be taboo in the Whittaker competition, for example. Some things are definitely distasteful. You could have a story about sexism, just as you could about extreme politics, but you'd have to write it carefully so you weren't promulgating a particular viewpoint that was considered illegal.

Similarly with violence: I read and write horror stories, and there are violent scenes in those. If they're just gratuitous blood-letting, then you'll find that the readers are turned off. In most competitions, the rules won't allow overt violence and sex scenes. Otherwise, there's nothing particularly taboo.

Piers Anthony, the science fiction writer, is an interesting case. He got into trouble for writing about consensual sex with a five-year-old girl. Now, I don't even want to *think* about that. Nevertheless, he did – and it got published. Most people didn't like it at all, and told him they weren't going to read his work again. I think there was also an attempt to take him to court that failed.

It would be a mistake to write stories that are going to get people's backs up so much. And you're not going to win many competitions that way. So you do have to be careful about what you're writing.

40. What turns a judge off?

[D] You must have seen a few bad entries in your time. What really turns you off?

[G] In the first two rounds of the 2009 Whittaker competition, there were several stories about relationships that had gone wrong. It was either about a husband who was overbearing and his wife eventually left, mutilated or killed him, or vice versa.

Several were about a single parent using a mobile phone a lot, bringing up her children on her own, and holding down a complicated professional job. This is also the theme of many television programmes, so I don't want to see it in short stories as well, and especially not in competitions.

Those are the sort of overdone tropes that turn me off – unless they have something extra to lift them above the others.

41. Tense and viewpoint

[D] Do you think stories need to be told in the past tense? Would you discount something told in the present tense?

[G] Again, it depends on the story. Some stories are much better in the first-person present tense because it gives them immediacy, but that doesn't allow much time for reflection, or for back story to be put in, except by cunning.

Third-person past tense is probably the most widely used for that reason; you can play around with it more, and you can use another character's point of view.

42. Location

[D] Do you think an exotic location enhances a story?

[G] Yes. But having said that, you can have a good story with a strange – and initially featureless – location. For example, Jean-Paul Sartre's *No Exit* is set in a room with four blank walls. It's entirely character-driven: emotions and personal conflicts.

The location is not the be-all and end-all of the story, but it can help to set the reader in an interesting frame of mind – as well as the story itself.

43. The judging process

[D] Did you send your feedback directly to the writers, or did someone else get to look at it first?

[G] I didn't know who the writers were as the organisers had removed their names before passing the stories on to me. I sent my feedback directly to the organisers, and they sent it to the writers at the end of the two weeks, so everyone received it at the same time.

[D] Did you read each story in full? Or did you cut corners? If, for example, there was a no-hoper and it was obvious from the first page, would you bother reading the rest of it?

[G] I had to read it all, because one of the judging categories was for the ending. There were very few no-hopers in that competition because they were all good writers.

I do recall an incident that involved a judge for the Man Booker Prize, in which he was on a train crossing Argentina and he had a heavy bag full of the longlist novels – which of course were all hardback at that point. He would read the first few pages of as many as he could. If the first five pages didn't grab him, he threw it out of the window. When he arrived in London, some of the books he'd hurled at the Aberdeen Angus out on the pampas were on the shortlist! So he had to have them sent to him again.

Not that I was in that sort of situation, but I always read all the stories right to the end.

[D] Do you read them at normal reading speed? Do you ever read a bit faster or skim through them if they look as if they're not too good?

[G] I might feel tempted to skim if it's a long one, but 2,500 words isn't that long. You're only talking about seven double-spaced pages, so they're short enough to read all in one go.

I pace myself too; the stories don't all come to me at once. Luckily, the organisers, Donna Gagnon and Doug Pugh, send me the stories as they receive them. Although there may be a rush near the deadline, I receive a few dribbles of stories during the couple of weeks beforehand. So even with the ones that I realise aren't going to win that round, I can take my time reading and critiquing them.

[D] Did you like being a judge, and would you do it again?

[G] Yes, I very much enjoyed being a judge and I would do it again. But I think it's a policy of the Whittaker Prize to have a different judge each year. That's fair enough, because after all, I have my biases, and it wouldn't be fair to the writers' development if they got the same sort of judgements each time.

But you need to have the time to be able to do it, a certain amount of stamina, and reliability, in the sense that you have to be consistent throughout it all.

It's probably a good thing for a judge to have editing skills, and to be widely read – and to be widely read as a writer as well. You should read with a writer's eye.

[D] What are the best and worst aspects of being a judge?

[G] The best aspect is the joy of encountering a great story – and there have been some brilliant ones.

The worst aspect is having to mark somebody low when you know they must have put a lot of effort in, but it just didn't cut it. Sometimes there was so much looseness in there, and you just knew you had to mark it low. Worse than that is when you get consecutive stories that are low-scoring, and you're wondering to yourself, "what's going on here?"

There are prompts for the Whittaker Prize – three prompts for each round. They don't have to use them if they don't feel inspired by them, which is quite a good thing. They get a photograph, a quotation, and a video clip from YouTube – so they get three different media. And I can tell if they've used them. Sometimes, I'll get a flurry of stories about a dog, for example, so I know that if I look through the prompts myself I can see that, oh yes, there it is. That's quite fun. So, yes, there are a lot of joys and benefits to being a judge.

[D] What do you like most about judging short stories? And what do you like least about it?

[G] The most pleasurable aspect is dipping into other people's ideas. Not to pinch their ideas; that hasn't actually happened – although I thought it might. They've written marvellous stories, but about aspects of life that I wouldn't write about. I've had the enormous pleasure of benefiting, especially, from their characters. I've seen characters who deserve a series of their own.

What I like least is the time it takes to judge, but we all complain that we haven't got enough time.

44. What if you disagree with the judge's assessment?

[D] If you, as a writer, disagree with a judge's assessment of your story, what should you do about it? Perhaps you should do nothing?

[G] I would sometimes have to go to a quiet room and have a think about it. It's just another person's opinion when it comes down to it.

At the Whittaker Prize, because it's part of *The Write Idea* forum, at the end of each round the winning story would be posted up, and the other competitors would be allowed to comment on it. My comments would also be put up, and they could then say things like, "I don't understand why he said that", and I could respond to that if I wanted. So, I was getting feedback on my feedback and the other competitors were commenting on *that* too.

I was advised by the organisers not to get too much involved with commenting on other people's comments about my comments. Nevertheless, I did sometimes. For example, if they couldn't understand why I marked a story low in a certain category, then it was only fair to explain my marking. I'm quite happy to justify my scores.

Many of the writers who didn't win also posted up their stories, along with their marks and my comments. On the whole, although some people disagreed with my comments, most of them found them helpful. I've had many letters since saying how helpful they found my critiques to be, because they hadn't fully considered certain aspects of writing that I had.

In the end, it's still my opinion – and just one person's opinion. One way that my being a judge helped them was that I tried to be consistent throughout the whole competition. In the end I think that was helpful.

It is a two-way perception and sometimes somebody would say, "Well, I don't understand why you didn't understand what I was getting at". Occasionally, the communication error was on the part of the writer, who hadn't written their ideas very well, and I, as a judge, didn't "get it". So that was a learning process for them too.

45. Are winners offered contracts by publishers and agents?

[D] I've heard that publishers and agents sometimes contact the winners of the bigger competitions and propose that they write a novel. Is there any truth in that?

[G] It has been known. Some of my friends in the science fiction world who have won some of the *prestigious* science fiction short story contests *have* been contacted by agents and asked to submit a novel. So it can work like that, yes. It's worth entering short story competitions for that reason.

46. Short stories as a stepping stone to novels

[D] With that in mind then, would you recommend short story competitions as a stepping stone to other writing, such as novels?

[G] I would, but there's a "but" in the answer. They are quite different things, a short story and a novel.

For example, with a short story, especially one up to about 2,500 words, you ought to have no more than two or three main characters. In a novel you can easily have five or six main characters, plus other sub-characters.

You should only have one point of view in a short story of 2,500 words. Having more means that the reader gets distracted and can't engage quite so much with just one of the characters. With a novel you can have several points of view – unless it's a first-person point of view novel, in which case you should stay with that all the way through.

These rules are broken all the time by famous writers. But if you're a budding writer hoping to become famous then it's wise to know all the rules before you break them.

Some authors write good short stories, but it doesn't seem to work quite so well for them in novel-length works. Again, one of those examples, to me, is A. L. Kennedy. Her best works, in my opinion, are her collections of short stories. She's written some longer novels, and it doesn't seem to quite work. That's partly because her strength is in her sensory show. When you apply that to a long novel, your head tends to get weary with so many metaphors and similes.

On the other hand, many novelists are also short story writers, and many of them became novelists by writing short stories in the first place. They did that partly to test the ground – to see how other people felt about their characters.

One of my other favourite novelists is Howard Waldman, especially his novel *Back There*, which is a brilliant literary novel about an American living in Paris – and by chance he *is* an American living in Paris. He used to place his short stories in forums to test the water with other critiquers, to see if a particular character possessed anything worthy of basing a novel around.

So the answer is yes – but be careful out there. Also, be aware that many magazines and anthologies consider placing a story online in forums, blogs or social media as publication. They might disallow it from a competition, or from publication with them, on the grounds that it has already been published.

47. Submission guidelines

[D] Here's another question from a member of the ideas4writers Facebook group. If you're sending a printed entry by post, should you send it by recorded delivery?

[G] No, because that means somebody has to be at the other end to sign for it. What happens if they aren't there? It goes back to the Post Office, and the organisers are then supposed to collect it later. They're just not going to do that.

Some competitions which accept printed entries allow you to enclose a stamped, self-addressed postcard. They'll fill it in, or stamp the date on it, and send it back to you as confirmation that they've received your entry.

With an email-only competition like the Whittaker, the organisers send competitors a confirmation that their entry has been received. The other way of checking that your entry has arrived is if there's an active online forum linked to the competition.

There are, unfortunately, some competitions that don't allow you *any* sort of knowledge that your entry has been received. It's just down to luck then.

[D] So you can't even include a stamped, self-addressed postcard with your entry?

[G] No. Some of them don't allow it.

[D] And you obviously wouldn't recommend phoning or emailing them in that case?

[G] I wouldn't. It's best not to annoy people. I wouldn't be irritated, as I'm such a soft touch, but I know that some competition organisers get annoyed with being pestered by competitors. It tends to be the same contestants time and again. They're always asking: has it been received?, was it formatted correctly?, and so on. The organisers prefer it if you just send it in and be patient.

48. The best time in your career to enter competitions

[D] Do you think people should start entering competitions as soon as they take up writing, in order to gain feedback? Or should they gain experience first, or take a creative writing course?

[G] In my view, they *shouldn't* enter competitions straight away. They may well get disheartened by not winning, or coming bottom.

If you're just about to start writing, it's best to join a critique group first, and test the waters with them. It's no good thinking you're a good writer because your auntie likes what you've written. Is she a writer or an editor? If so, then fair enough. Otherwise I would gain experience first.

Maybe take a creative writing course at your local college. Then join an online critique group to get feedback and learn how to improve your writing. Start entering competitions once your feedback is consistently good and you've got rid of most of your writing gremlins.

49. Advice for beginners

[D] **Do you have any other advice for someone who wants to start writing short stories?**

[G] It's a glib thing to say, but to be a good writer you should learn to be a good reader. There's a difference between being a good reader and reading something as a writer. In other words, once you know about clichés, point of view, show not tell, and so on, then you read things differently.

I belong to a real-life readers' group – in fact I'm the only bloke in one group, and I get to take a different woman home each time. Unfortunately, my wife knows them all, so...

Anyway, the interesting thing is that these women are all intellectual, and they're all much more widely read than me, except possibly in my own genre of science fiction. When I talk about point of view, or about show not tell, I have to explain to them what I mean. They hadn't noticed these aspects of fiction.

People who are just casual readers for pleasure often don't notice things that writers and editors do. Unfortunately, when you're entering competitions, the people judging them are generally people with editorial and/or writing experience – except for celebrity judges of course. They *are* looking for the aspects of writing that we're all supposed to adhere to.

You should also read how-to books. There are plenty of them: how to write short stories and novels and so on. I wouldn't say any particular one of them is better than the others. One of my favourite books on writing generally is *On Writing* by Stephen King. It's not specifically about short stories, but he's written plenty of them so that aspect does come into it.

50. Learning from competition winners

[D] Where can people find prize-winning stories so they can read them for themselves and learn from them?

[G] Most competitions publish an anthology of their winning stories. Often the top three stories from each round, say, will get published in an anthology. Sometimes that's a print anthology, or sometimes it's online. Often the online ones can be downloaded free of charge. So you can certainly read winning stories that way.

And there are plenty of others: the Bridport Prize publishes anthologies of their winning entries. They aren't always available in high street newsagents or bookshops, but sometimes they are, so it's worth searching for them there.

[D] Or have a look at the competition organiser's own website, which will almost certainly have it.

Is there any way that people can read the judge's comments on those stories?

[G] That's tricky. Many competitions run a forum or social media site alongside the competition. Some of them will publish the judge's comments for the winning entries. Or individual competitors will do that. But some won't because they're embarrassed. For example, in my comments I might point out an aspect of their writing, and they would then write back to me and say what an idiot they felt because it's something *they* would point out to other people, but they'd made the same mistake themselves. Also, they might not then wish those comments to be read by their peers in the forum. Feedback is the property of the competitor, and they might not want it all made public.

The FicFun website[1], whose competition I judged, is a writing showcase. Writers often put up a story one chapter or section at a time, allowing readers to comment. Other people can read those.

[D] The winning stories that are published in the writing magazines usually include a few comments from the judge. Though I have to say the ones I've seen weren't always helpful. For example, many of them were simply short extracts of the

story that the judge said were particularly good. But there was no explanation as to why he felt they were good.

[1] http://ficfun.com

51. The keys to success

[D] Is there an easy way to write a great short story?

[G] No. There's no easy way to write any sort of good writing at all. It's all hard work. It becomes easier if you work at it, and you read the how-to guides, and you look at all the advice on the web about how to write good stories. But there isn't an easy way to do it.

You have to have a good hook and good characters, make it tight and cut out the pleonasms, and swing in with some stunning idea halfway through the story. It's not easy. I don't think we'll ever say it is.

[D] What do you think is the key to becoming a successful short story writer?

[G] Read your words out loud. It's absolutely critical. Everything you write. Preferably read it into a microphone and record it. Leave it an hour or two – or a day or two if you're patient enough – and then listen to it again.

Reading it aloud, even if it's to yourself or to your cat or dog, you'll be amazed how it will make you want to change it.

[D] What would you say is the next step after winning a short story competition? Enter more competitions? Try the more prestigious ones? Go for the bigger prizes? Publication for payment? Write a novel?

[G] I wouldn't leap into writing a novel straight away. As I explained earlier, writing a novel is quite different from writing short stories, and even winning a competition. If your short story was such that you could see how it could easily extend to a novel – and many of them can – then fair enough, give it a go.

Consider entering more competitions. Go for bigger markets too – the bigger and more expensive competitions – and have a go at submitting your stories to paying markets. There are so many. I think almost all the genres are covered these days by websites such as www.ralan.com/m.pro.htm

They'll tell you what markets are available at the moment, what sort of magazines, how much they pay, what sort of things they're looking for, and they have a link to all their websites.

Whether you're entering competitions or trying for the paying markets, you should always have several stories out there circulating all the time.

53. Don't do these things

[D] What do you recommend that people do *not* do?

[G] You must not copy. Having said that, there's no reason why you couldn't get *inspiration* from other people's work, and by being widely read, liking their ideas, and knowing how you could take that idea in another direction or give it another dimension somewhere.

Unfortunately there *have* been people copying, and it's been happening recently. There are accusations of plagiarism on the web, and with some of the web-based short story competitions. These cases have been well publicised, and they could go to court. You must never plagiarise somebody else's writing.

Another thing you should *not* do in short stories is to have more than one point of view. And stick to no more than two or three main characters. With the "unless it works really well" proviso for those last two points.

54. How to start writing a story

[D] Can you tell me how you, personally, start writing a story?

[G] For me the plot comes first. Or at least the main element of a plot, the idea – usually something bizarre.

My stories tend to be about fairly ordinary people, but to whom extraordinary things happen. It's a sub-genre known as magical realism. In other words, they're not things you'd normally see in everyday life, but supposing you *did*! Then what?

For example, a recent short story I wrote, called *View From*[1], was critiqued at Café Doom, and also by the British Science Fiction Association's[2] critique group, called Orbiters. Suppose you woke up one morning and you were stuck on the ceiling. What would your view of the world be like then? How did you get there? Who are you? Who lives on the floor above you that might have organised this thing? What does your girlfriend say when she comes in and sees you up there on the ceiling? It's bizarre, but just suppose it happened. It was just a short story, but it was fun to write.

The characters have to come next. I have to appreciate that although they're ordinary people with extraordinary things happening to them, they can't be *too* ordinary, otherwise they'd lack interest.

[1] You can read Geoff's story *View From* at the end of this book.

[2] www.bsfa.co.uk

55. Geoff's experience as a writer, competitor and judge

[D] **You mentioned earlier that you've entered competitions yourself. Can you tell me which ones they were and how you got on?**

[G] Well, just like you, I first started writing as a child. I entered and won a couple of competitions back then. I didn't keep any records.

It wasn't until about fifteen years ago that I started writing seriously and started keeping a CV and records.

In more recent times, I won the Writers of the Future contest, which is one of the science fiction short story competitions. More recently, Café Doom ran regular competitions and I won two of those. I was a runner-up in one or two others. In the spring of 2018 my science fiction short story *Angular Size* was shortlisted by the British Science Fiction Association for their best shorter story. It was a poll vote and I just missed the top prize, but it was an honour to be highly placed and the story was republished in an anthology.

My novels have had commendations. *Exit, Pursued by a Bee* came second in a Preditors and Editors Reader's Poll. My novel *Hot Air* won a gold award for best unpublished novel from a Dutch Arts Academy. *ARIA: Left Luggage* won the Preditors and Editors Poll for best science fiction novel of 2012.

[D] What would you say is the most important thing you've learnt about writing short stories from judging them?

[G] The importance of character over plot – even though, as I said, the latter comes first in my planning. I used to believe that plot was more important than character. Indeed, you'll find that same view in some of the how-to books, such as Della Galton's *How to Write and Sell Short Stories*. I'm beginning to disagree with that. Although you do need a hook and a conflict in every story, it's the characters that drive it.

[D] What do you wish you had known when you first started writing short stories?

[G] The first thing is to write it much tighter. That still applies even now, and I've been writing seriously for over twenty years. My most recent published novel is a fantasy called *Xaghra's Revenge*. It took me years to write and polish it, but if I were to pick any page at random now, I'd still find a way of tightening it more. It never stops.

Also, you need to make the characters over-the-top. It's no good having a "nice" person. They can be a pleasant person, but they've got to have some flaw. All characters have to have a flaw, even if it's an amusing or pleasant trait.

And every story must have conflict, otherwise there's nothing to resolve – no real story.

I'd say those were the three things that I wish I'd known umpteen years ago, instead of just appreciating them more and more all the time now.

[D] What (or who) first inspired you to start writing?

[G] My mother was a keen reader, especially of science fiction and historical novels. She joined me into the Children's Science Fiction Book Club when I was four, so I had that in my blood. My father used to illustrate science fiction magazines back in the 1950s. So I just thought everybody did it!

Then when I went to school, they wanted people to write skits, to pretend they were as good as *Monty Python* and *That Was The Week That Was*. I was the one they picked to do that – writing quips. That continued right up until university. I helped edit the Sheffield University rag mag, *Twikker*, during the late 60s and early 70s. Some of those awful rag mag jokes are mine – I have the royalties. (I don't actually – I might have had the copyright, but no royalties! Of course, it's all for charity anyway.) So that's how I started writing – just writing jokes and quips.

[D] What important lesson did you learn from your first writings?

[G] Something important for all writers: that there wasn't a universal dislike of my writing. People did seem to like my jokes, corny though they were. So that gave me the urge to continue.

[D] How do you write your stories? Do you write them straight onto a computer? And when it comes to editing, do you do that on your computer, or do you print it out?

[G] I always write directly onto the computer these days – partly because my handwriting's pretty awful. That's why I learnt to touch type while I was at university.

For the editing, I prefer to read on paper. I find that if I print it out and take it somewhere quiet and read it there, then I can read it out loud more easily, and other things like the commas and full stops are easier to see too. It's the same for judging competitions. It's the same for book reviews too. The only book reviews I'll do on screen are for pre-publication reviews when they need what's called a "puff quote" to go on the back cover.

[D] Where do you do most of your writing?

[G] Most of my writing is done at home in a comfortable armchair with a keyboard on my lap and the screen an arm's length away. I quite enjoy writing like that.

But I'll write anywhere. I have a small laptop that slips into my rucksack or cycle pannier if I'm going hiking or cycling anywhere and stopping at a Youth Hostel. It's quite nice to be able to write a story in the location it's set in.

I wrote a short story, *Camera Shy*, about the Place de la Concorde in Paris, France, and I wrote that while sitting in an outdoor café in that very place. It's rare, of course, that you can do that, but, yes – have laptop, will travel!

56. Recommended writing software

[D] Do you use any software to help you compose, write, organise or edit your stories?

[G] I was brought up with Microsoft Word, right from when it was a DOS program. Many people complain about it, but you get used to often-used programs and their quirks. Word has a lot of nice features, which I'm still learning.

The only thing that annoys me about it is that the word count is based on an assumption that every word is something like five characters long. So it isn't an accurate count of the number of words you've typed. If you try and count all the words in a novel one by one you're bound to get it wrong. Or if you do an averaging out, based on the number of pages and lines and so on, that's going to be out too.

[D] That's interesting. I use Word too, but I hadn't heard about the problem with the word count.

Have you tried any of the programs that help you build a plot and characters, and so on?

[G] I have tried other programs – NewNovelist[1] is quite an interesting one. I tried it when it first came out, and I was quite intrigued by it, especially with the aspects of being able to do plotting ideas before writing the story. I didn't like it in the end though. So I just use Word now.

[D] I tried NewNovelist too when it first came out. It must have been around the same time that you did. I remember writing a scathing review of it. I know a lot of other writers had bad experiences with it – crashes, losing their work, lack of support, and so on. But that was version 1, and it's been updated several times since then, and it's still around, so perhaps it's much better now. But I haven't ever gone back to it.

I've tried a few others such as Scrivener, WriteItNow, Writer's Café, StoryWeaver, Writer's Dream Kit, and Dramatica Pro but I've always come back to Microsoft Word in the end. That's all I use for writing now. But I have a couple of apps on my iPad that I wouldn't want to be without: SimpleMind+ for mind maps and WorkFlowy for outlining.

For plotting novels, I use a twenty-year-old book called *The Marshall Plan for Novel Writing* by Evan Marshall. I have the accompanying workbook too. I swear at them every time I use them though, because they never take you quite far enough. They take you past the halfway point of plotting your novel, but then leave you to finish the rest of it yourself before you feel you've got all the plot points and information you need. I guess the author didn't want to be too prescriptive. But I want him to be *more* prescriptive!

[G] If I'm away and I have the urge to do some writing and I haven't got my own computer, I'll quite happily use another word processing program, whether it's OpenOffice[2] or WordPerfect or Wordpad or Google Docs or something else. I'll use anything – whatever is available. I'll even use a writing app on my smartphone, though my fingers get in the way.

[D] I've got Microsoft Word on my iPad, which I usually take with me if I'm going anywhere. I tried using Google Docs on my iPad while I was at the library, but it didn't save the file properly and I lost several hours' work. So I just stick to Word now.

[G] I've sometimes used Microsoft Excel to organise chapters and to make a spreadsheet of the number of pages and number of words in each chapter. I've come to realise that people don't like long chapters – as some people have known for a long time. All of my chapters have been too long. I don't think Dan Brown invented short chapters, but certainly one of his chapters has only three words in it, so he must have the record for that.

Out of interest, I asked my readers' group about this. They were unanimous about wanting short chapters that can be easily read at bedtime. So I've sometimes used software, such as the tables in Word, or an Excel spreadsheet, to help me sort out how many words are in the chapters, and where they are, and so on.

[D] I used Excel in a different way when I wrote one of my novels. I gave each scene an excitement score, where 1 was a calm, reflective scene and 10 was all-guns-blazing edge-of-your-seat stuff. Then I plotted it on a graph using Excel, so I could get a visual overview of the story and move scenes around to improve the flow.

I also really like one of the features of Word's outline function – and it's the same in the WorkFlowy app on my iPad – where you can compress each scene or chapter into a single line. You can get a fantastic overview of your story that way, and move things around really easily.

To make things easier, I also give each scene a title. I remove the titles from the final manuscript, but they help me a lot while I'm writing and organising the story.

[1] www.newnovelist.com
[2] www.openoffice.org

57. Practice makes perfect

[D] How many of your stories would you say are good? And how many do you now regard as just a learning exercise, even though you might have thought they were good at the time?

[G] I've written about two hundred stories, of which I think about twenty probably are good. I think some people might like some of the other stories because they particularly like the theme. Of the twenty that I think are good, I wouldn't say any of them couldn't be improved.

There are some stories that you write and you fall in love with somehow, even though other people might not reckon they're your best work. I particularly enjoyed writing a story called *Prime Meridian*, which I wrote many years ago and is featured in an anthology called *Dimensions*. It's being republished later this year in a new anthology called *INCREMENTAL*.

[D] When you started writing, how long was it until you first got published or won anything?

[G] I got published almost straight away, because I was a student at the time. I had a story and a non-fiction article published in the first issue of the student magazine for the North Gloucestershire Technical College – which is now Cheltenham University. I didn't know anything about writing in those days, except plot. I didn't know about point of view, show not tell, or characterisation. But I had a good story! That's all the editors knew about too, luckily, because they were also students.

It was quite a long time before I got a story published by a *proper* magazine that was edited by people who knew what they were doing. That was when I was still a teacher. *Crystal* was the magazine – which is a literary magazine. I got a story printed in that decades after my first publication in a student magazine.

58. Getting ideas

[D] Apart from the ideas4writers books, where do you get your ideas from?

[G] From many different places – like most writers. I go cycling and hiking on my own, and I get many ideas popping into my head while wandering. I have a theory that all that extra activity oxygenates my brain more, so it activates that one little creative cell!

Other ideas come from reading magazines like *New Scientist* – because I'm a science fiction writer – and from dreams. You need to be careful with dreams. One tip, if you like, is to not use dreams in your writing. It's been done so much that it's become a cliché. So try to avoid dreams – especially if it was the explanation for all the conflict in the story.

Overheard comments often give rise to quite good stories – especially if you're hard of hearing like I am, so I *mishear* comments.

For example, the writer Ruth Hamilton was on the phone to me a few years ago and I was sure she said that somebody was a ghost before he died. Now, of course, you can't be a ghost before you've died, you have to be a ghost afterwards – or so the theory goes. But I liked the idea of somebody being a ghost before they died, so that ended up being a story. I wrote it that night – and sold it that night too. The funny thing is, when I asked Ruth about it afterwards, she had no recollection at all of ever having said the words "a ghost before he died".

News items give rise to good stories. You can often just change them a little, or even use them as they are. Sometimes the news is too bizarre to use in a story though. Here's one of the best news items I ever came across. I haven't seen it in fiction yet, though I'm amazed; maybe it's because the story itself sounds fictional.

A Zimbabwe bus driver was driving a group of patients to a psychiatric hospital. He stopped, not at a bus stop, but at a café to grab refreshments for himself. When he returned to his bus, it was empty. All of his patients had gone for a walk. He drove around for a while looking for them, but he couldn't find them. He came to another bus stop and there were about twenty people waiting for their bus. So he told them he was the bus they were waiting for, let them all on board ... and then he locked the doors and drove them to the psychiatric hospital.

The passengers were upset about this, of course, but he had locked them in the bus. He went into the hospital and explained to the staff that these passengers were their patients. They would of course protest and try to deny it – but that's what happens with psychiatric patients. It was two weeks before the last of those bus passengers was finally released.

Now, how hilarious is that, even if it's apocryphal, and why hasn't it featured in a short story somewhere yet? So, yes, keep looking out for the news.

There are so many places to get ideas from. The ideas4writers books you do, and the What Ifs in *The Fastest Way to Get Ideas* are a goldmine of stories. So definitely go for those.

[D] When you're judging competitions, do you spot ideas for stories you could write yourself, or gaps in the market?

[G] When I read the prompts in some of the competitions, it stirs different ideas for me than it does for some of the competitors. I see characters in some of the competitors' stories that I haven't seen anywhere else. So there's a sort of character gap in the market, in a way. I mentioned this to one writer. I said, "Look, you've got two old women in that story who are so brilliant they ought to have a series of their own". I don't know about any gaps in the market as such, though. Not that occur to me anyway.

59. Writing novels as a next step

[D] As well as short stories, you also write novels. Can you tell me more about those?

[G] I had the urge to write novels from when I was a teenager onwards, but being a teacher, it was difficult to fit it in. Nevertheless, I did write two novels while I was a teacher. One of them was a science fiction story based on a *Jurassic Park*-type situation – before Michael Crichton thought of it. It involved fossilised plants that were regenerated, with genetic modification, from seeds found in amber. A CND group used them as little plant bombs around nuclear silos in America, Russia and England. They were so successful that they didn't stop growing, and nothing could kill them. So imagine a nice end-of-the-Earth-type apocalyptic story based on that. I submitted it to several publishers, and one of them, Bloomsbury, *nearly* published it.

I was horrified that they didn't want to publish it in the end. I didn't realise how lucky I was that it had passed through something like five committee stages. One of the editors wrote me a five-page critique, even quoting bits he liked.

Strangely enough, Michael Crichton worked at Bloomsbury at that time as one of their staff writers. So you never know, maybe he saw my story, which was called *Convolvulus* – because the plant that got out of control was based on a convolvulus (bindweed) plant. He may have thought, "I can do better than this". And so he did, with *Jurassic Park*.

Although *Convolvulus* wasn't published, I reused the idea for a chapter in my novel *ARIA: Left Luggage*, in which a convolvulus-hybrid plant gets out of control, eventually forcing the surviving humans to abandon the planet.

My first published novel was *Escaping Reality*, a humorous thriller. It was a story that was always in me – a British version of the TV series *The Fugitive*. It was a little similar to *The 39 Steps* but brought up to date. It's more of a humour story than a thriller, but there's no such thing as a humorous thriller in the genres publishers use. So they didn't want it for that reason, until a small press publisher, Brambling Books, took it on. It sold quite well – I think about 2,000 copies altogether have been sold since 2004. It's been improved – especially after you, Dave, bought a copy and sent me pages of corrections, for which I was grateful. That was part of my learning curve. You never stop learning as a writer, and I certainly learnt a lot from writing that one. That book is still available, though only on Kindle now.

After that I wrote *Hot Air*, then I started writing science fiction. I've written science fiction short stories for years – all my life almost – but *Exit, Pursued by a Bee* appealed to me as it has some ideas contrary to the norm. I wanted aliens that were already here, but leaving. I wanted aliens leaving in their machines, but slowly. No roaring away at escape velocity, but just slowly taking off. I really liked that idea.

I also liked the idea of having aliens that wouldn't communicate with Earth people. Maybe they couldn't; maybe they didn't use radio, they used some other means. So I had to invent a means of communication that we don't use. I chose a quantum physics methodology using time decoherence. Time decoherence is where atoms, in their fluctuations, change time in microscopic ways. I used that to make a new form of communication. So I had great fun with that. Double Dragon Publishing was good enough to publish it in the summer of 2008. It's still available – and selling quite well. There's a nice video trailer out for it. Search for *Exit, Pursued by a Bee* on YouTube. (Not the famous "Exit, pursued by a bear" stage direction in *A Winter's Tale*.)

I've also written *ARIA*, a science fiction trilogy based on an original premise of alien retrograde infectious amnesia.

And *Xaghra's Revenge* is a fantasy based on the real-life abduction of the entire population of Gozo by pirates in 1551. All their spirits seek revenge. So that's where I'm up to with my books.

[D] Where can people go to find out more about you and your work?

[G] They can go to any of the online bookstores and type in Geoff Nelder and they'll find my books and pieces there. Or they can go to my website which is www.geoffnelder.com – all the links are there, with information about each of the books and some sample short stories.

60. The final secret

[D] Finally, Geoff, is there one big secret about writing short stories, or judging them, that you wouldn't normally share with anyone – or if you did you'd have to kill them?

[G] Everybody's looking for this big secret – including me – and I would say, along with Noah Lukeman, that in order to have something special, it has to transcend the normal short story.

It has to have something that lifts readers out of their everyday lives; a facet that clicks with them; some imagery; excellent writing; and use of sensory show where appropriate.

Also, for me, somewhere about two-thirds of the way through the story, it's got to have a sideways kick that you didn't expect. Not necessarily a twist at the end – though that can be good – but something special that's going to knock you about and make you want to read it again.

Bonus Section

1. Dave's comments from judging the ideas4writers short story competitions.

2. Short story with judge's comments from the 2009 Whittaker Prize: *Return to Cairo* by Jonathan Pinnock.

3. Short story: *View From* by Geoff Nelder.

Dave's comments from judging the ideas4writers short story competitions

I want to point out the most common and most glaring errors I came across while judging the ideas4writers short story competitions.

- Punctuation, grammar and basic sentence construction are extremely important. Please learn how to do it or you'll get rejected every time and you'll never win a competition. Spend an evening reading a pocket-guide and your writing will improve instantly.

- Double-check every occurrence of "its" and "it's" and make sure you've used the right one.

- Paragraphs: yes, you do need them. And that means pressing the Return key just once, not twice.

- Do not leave a blank line between paragraphs. Only do this between scenes – to indicate the passing of time, a change of location, or a change of viewpoint character, for example.

- The first line of each paragraph should be indented – use the Tab key rather than typing several spaces, or set your word processor to indent paragraphs automatically. But do not indent the first line of the story, or the first line of a new scene or section.

- Paragraphs should usually be much less than a page long, especially if you're writing for children. A new paragraph every five to seven sentences would be a good idea. But try to have a few longer and shorter ones so it looks more interesting on the page, and less intimidating to read.

- Sentences that are more than thirty words long are also not a good idea. I saw some with more than sixty.

- A sentence should contain only one thought, idea or action, not several strung together and separated by commas (or, worse, not separated at all).

- Older British writers should also check that the actions are in the correct (i.e. chronological) sequence. For some reason – and it's very, *very* common – older people in Britain have a tendency to construct their sentences back to front, with the last action stated first and the first action stated last – and it doesn't make any sense. I see this a lot when editing books too. I assume it must have been taught that way in schools many years ago. But it's wrong. You don't see it in books or newspapers that were published back then, so I'm not really sure what the schools were thinking.

- You need to begin a new paragraph each time somebody different starts speaking.

- Do not use full justification (both left and right margins aligned). Things are printed that way in books and magazines, but it's not how it should look when you submit it to an editor or competition judge. Full justification makes it difficult to tell how much space a story or article will take up in a magazine, and it's impossible to tell whether extra spaces have been added by accident. So please use left justification only.

- Read your story aloud to yourself – or to your pets if you like – and ask a couple of literate (and highly pedantic) people to proofread it before you send it off. The errors will become strikingly obvious when you do this.

- Unless you're using the omniscient point of view – which I don't recommend – decide whose point of view you're using, and stick to it. If your main character is a child, for example, and you're letting your readers see what he's thinking, then you shouldn't also reveal what his mother or aunt are thinking – and especially not within the same paragraph. You can say that it looked as if his mother was angry, or she sounded angry, but you can't reveal her exact thoughts, worries, and so on, as if we were inside her head.

If you wanted to do that, you would have to start a new scene and make her the viewpoint character, so we see everything from her perspective – and only hers. You wouldn't be able to let your readers see things from the child's point of view during that scene.

Published writers break this rule all the time – which I find rather annoying. But if you're entering a competition it's definitely best to obey it.

- If the competition organisers give you the first sentence of the story then you must use that exact sentence. You can't change any of the words or edit the sentence in any way.

Some entrants in our competitions added speech marks to the sentence we provided and turned it into a piece of dialogue. We decided to allow this. However, judges of other competitions might not be so lenient, and it could get you disqualified.

Short story with judge's comments from the 2009 Whittaker Prize: *Return to Cairo* by Jonathan Pinnock

Please note that this story contains language that some readers may find offensive.

Judge's critique:

(The judge received the story anonymously)

> The voice is the strongest element in this story, with teen angst and behaviour, along with underlying passion and care, coming over very well. A mystery is set in the opening and is resolved by the end. The end is weak – I'd have liked the aunt at the funeral to reveal that Nan really meant Cairo to be a favourite café she used to visit in her youth on Kyle Row in Middleton, but there's me re-writing other people's stories. I would have thought even an über-busy mother would have been aware and shown more concern than the teens' mum in this tale. Afterwards is one word.

Marks on the Whittaker Prize scoring grid:

Story Title:	*Return to Cairo*
Opening (10):	8
Characters (15):	12
Inventiveness (20):	17
Voice (30):	25
Ending (15):	10
Technicalities (10):	9
TOTAL (100):	81

This story came joint second, only one point behind the leader of that round, in which twenty submissions were received.

After revision, Jon Pinnock submitted this story to another competition and received an award. In his own words: "I received your critique on May 19th, revised it and sent it off to the City of Derby competition on May 27th, just in time for the end of May deadline. It was awarded 3rd prize by Sara Maitland. I think the most important thing that you suggested was to sort out the ending so that the reference to Cairo was a bit more believable. I don't seem to have made any other changes – maybe I should have done!"

Return to Cairo
(revised version)
by Jonathan Pinnock

I catch Danny just as he's leaving for work. He's getting into that crappy little car of his when I call out to him, "Oi, Dans, get us some sand, will you? It's for Nan."

He shakes his head. "What? No way. I'm fucking late as it is, and Mario'll kill me."

Danny works in a shitty burger joint over in Middleton. I don't know why he doesn't get a better job. Well I do, really. It's because he's thick and lazy.

"Oh, please, Dans. For Nan."

"No. It's stupid, and anyway why can't you get Mum to get some?"

He really is dim sometimes. Mum works at Arkwrights all day long, packing stuff, and then she goes off to clean offices in the evenings. The rest of the time, she sleeps. All so's we can have a university education, she says. Well, Danny didn't take up the offer. Tosser.

"You know fucking well why I can't ask Mum."

"Don't swear, little sis," says Danny. "And I've got to go. So no deal." He starts to close the car door.

OK, time to play my ace. "You know Saffron Henderson?"

The door opens again like a shot. "What's it to you?"

"Her sister's in my class this year. Could put a word in for you."

You can almost see the cogs ticking. Finally, he rolls his eyes. "All right, then. I'll go to B&Q when I finish tonight."

"Good boy. Mind you get that nice smooth silver sand. The stuff they use in sandpits."

"Yeah, whatever." And he drives off, as fast as a twenty-year-old Micra can go, with black smoke belching out the back. He's such an embarrassment.

Still, mission accomplished.

"Your Nan still think she's in Cairo?" says Lorna Henderson, after she's agreed to make the introduction.

"Yeah."

"That's cool," she says. "Well, for her, anyway. Must be a nightmare for you lot."

"Yeah. It's weird as shit."

"Funny. I can't imagine my Nan ever going to Cairo."

"Me neither. I used to think the furthest she'd ever got from here was Margate. She never wanted to come to Spain with us, 'cos of the food."

"My Nan lives in a home. Don't think she's very happy there. Stinks of piss."

"Aw, that's sad."

"Yeah. I don't want to get old."

"Me neither."

"When my time's up, y'know what I want to do?" Lorna looks dreamy for a moment. "I want to jump out of a burning plane, naked, with no parachute, strapped to Johnny Depp."

We both snigger. The bell goes for the next lesson. Lorna's cool.

I don't know how we ended up with Nan living with us. It's hard enough for Mum coping with Danny and me, but Nan's getting more and more difficult all the time. Not that Mum notices. She's so tired when she gets in, she's in a little world of her own. It's me who ends up dealing with Nan. And I'm the one she says it to.

"Want to go back to Cairo."

"What? Can you lift your leg a bit more?" I'm trying to change her catheter bag. The district nurse explained to me how to do it, but I'm still getting the hang of it.

"I said I want to go back to Cairo. Liked it there."

"Nan, you've never been to Cairo," I say. "Have you?"

"Have. Nice place. Hot. Full of Arabs, y'know."

"Nan, you've never been abroad. You haven't even got a passport."

"Have."

"No you haven't."

"Want to go back to Cairo."

Danny thinks it's really funny. Which is surprising really, because I very much doubt if he has a clue where Cairo is.

"She keeps going on about it every time I'm in with her. If you spent more time with –"

"Watch it, sis. I've got a job to go to."

"And I've got homework to do."

"What's that?"

"Something you never bothered with, obviously."

"Listen, brainbox. I get my education at the University of Life. Worth far more than a fucking degree."

I'm just about to tell him that he'd probably fail to get a place even there, when the front door opens and Mum comes in. She looks tired as usual.

"When was Nan in Cairo, Mum?" I say.

"What?"

"Nan. In Cairo."

"Dunno. Never mentioned it to me. Why?"

"Says she wants to go back there."

Mum laughs. "Well, I'm not paying for the air fare."

Then I have my idea. It's a brilliantly simple idea. But when I explain it to Mum and Danny, they both think I'm the biggest idiot in Idiot Street in Idiot Town.

"Do what?" they both say.

I shrug. "I just meant we could pretend she's in Cairo. It's not much to do for her, is it?"

"But how?"

The first thing to do is turn the heating up. It's the beginning of summer anyway, but I get every heater in the house into Nan's room and switch them all on full.

"It's hot," she says.

"'Course it's hot, Nan. You're in a hot country."

"Where am I?"

"In Cairo, of course."

"Doesn't look like Cairo."

"That's because you're inside."

"Doesn't sound like Cairo."

"That's because –" Sod it. "You're not quite there yet," I say.

This is going to take a little more work than I'd bargained on. Next day after school, I go down to the library and have a look in the World Music section. Jesus, there's some weird stuff there, I can tell you. But I find this thing called "Arabian Moods" which looks promising. I take it home, and put it on in Nan's room, and she perks up a little.

"What's that?" she says.

"It's Egyptian music."

"Are we there yet?"

"Almost."

The next thing I do is sneak into Dan's room and nick some of that incense that his last girlfriend, Moonbeam, left behind. I know.

Don't worry. She didn't last long. Even he realised she was mental.

So we've got heat, music and incense. Nan is getting the full-on Middle Eastern ambience.

"Still don't think we're in Cairo," she says.

Lorna thinks we should have the call to prayer going out at regular intervals throughout the day. I'm not too sure how we'd manage this.

"You can get it piped in from the mosque, you know."

"Bollocks," I say.

"It's true. The Khans next door get it."

"How do you know?"

She rolls her eyes. "'Cos we hear it going off at five o'clock in the bleeding morning. The walls are dead thin."

"Oh. 'Spect you have to be a Muslim, though."

"Yeah. You could pretend you are."

"I don't think it's quite that simple."

"Nah. 'Spose not."

Then I show her my diagram. She bursts out laughing.

"You're kidding," she says.

"No. I'm dead serious."

"Well, if you really want that made, I know the bloke who can do it. He's a total geek, but he's ace at metalwork." She turns round towards an Asian kid in thick glasses who's sitting a few tables away. "Oi, Slumdog! Come here!" The boy glances nervously around and then heads over in our direction.

"This is Slumdog," she says. He winces. "Show him your picture," she says to me.

I give it to him. He gives a serious nod and then says, "When do you want it?"

"Er . . . you sure?"

"Of course. So when do you want it?"

"Er . . . next week?"

"Sure. No problem." He takes my piece of paper and goes off. "I think he likes you," says Lorna.

He turns out to be called Parthipan, and he's as good as his word. The machine that he comes up with is even better than I'd planned. Basically, you feed the sand into a chute at the top, and it slowly trickles through a tube until it hits the fan, at which point it gets scattered in all directions. When he brings it round, Nan is thrilled.

"We are in Cairo, aren't we?" she says when she gets the first few grains of sand in her face.

"Yes, we are." Although, to be honest, I'm getting more than a little sick of that Arabian Moods CD. I say so to Parthipan.

"What you need are some street sounds," he says.

"Could you do that?"

"Of course. Just need to find some effects somewhere and rig up the CD on continuous play. I'll see what I can do."

"What about the call to prayer? Could you rig that up too?"

"Hold on. Do you think I'm a Muslim or something?"

"Well, no," I say, "I s'pose you're a Hindu, but I thought –"

"I'm not even a Hindu."

"Really?"

"My parents are Christians. They're from Tamil Nadu in the south of India. A lot of the people there are Christians, you know."

"Oh."

Then, all of a sudden, Nan pipes up. "Oi, who's that Arab boy?"

We both freeze.

"Er . . . sorry, Nan?"

"The brown boy. Who's the Arab?"

I whisper to Parthipan, "I think she means you."

"No flipping way," he whispers back.

"Please?" This is embarrassing, but I really don't want to upset Nan. There is a look of panic in his eyes. I nudge him.

"Er . . . can I help you?" he says to Nan eventually.

"Do the accent," I hiss at him. He glares back at me. But to my amazement, he does try to put on a cod Middle Eastern accent, and I'm thinking this is so unbelievably wrong in so many different ways. In fact, he puts on a totally brilliant performance, and Nan laps it up.

"Thanks," I say to him as he is leaving.

"One thing," says Parthipan. "Please don't ever do that to me again. Ever."

But a week or so later, he's back. He needs to run some maintenance checks on the sand machine. He's also brought with him an MP3 player with a whole day's worth of street sounds that he's put together, including – woo hoo! – the call to prayer at regular intervals. He also tells me that a friend of a friend reckons he can get hold of a dodgy Sky box with a free subscription to Al Jazeera. I haven't a clue what Al Jazeera is, so he tells me that it's basically Channel Al Qa'eda.

"Cool," I say. Nan'll like that. I've been busy too. I've decided to supplement Nan's meals with some Middle Eastern extras. Actually, all I've managed to get hold of so far are some things called Falafels, and she doesn't like them much. Too greasy.

Anyway, Parthipan's just about to leave when Nan notices him again. This time, he tries to make for the door before he gets asked to perform, but it's too late. She calls out to him, "Oi! You! Arab boy! Come here and talk to me." He gives me a pleading look, and then gives in.

"What can I do for you, Miss?" he says, going over to her.

"Well, you can tell me one thing for a start," she says. "Why don't you wear Egyptian dress like all the other boys?"

If looks could kill. Because he knows exactly what I'm thinking.

There's a bit of an atmosphere between us when Parthipan leaves. As he's going out of the front door, Danny comes back in.

"Who's your boyfriend?" he says.

"Piss off," I say.

It's called a djellaba, and it's dead easy to make out of a couple of old sheets. I ask Parthipan if I can measure him up, but he puts his foot down this time. He says it's insulting. And I sort of begin to see his point. But he still comes round quite often to talk to Nan. I think he quite likes her, although she says some really dodgy things to him. Sometimes I try to tell her that she can't say that, but I suppose things were different in her day.

One day, Parthipan invites me round his house and I get to meet his mum and dad. They're really nice, and his mum cooks some wicked food. She tells me that she thinks what I'm doing for Nan is really good, and she says it's so nice to see me caring for her like that. So many of you white people just put their old people in homes, she says, and then she seems a bit embarrassed for saying it. But I know what she means.

"What are you up to with Slumdog?" says Lorna.

"None of your business," I say. "And don't call him Slumdog. It's racist."

"No it isn't."

"Yes it is, and anyway his name's Parthipan."

"Well if I was called something stupid like Parthipan I wouldn't worry about being called Slumdog."

"Yeah, well you're stupid and all."

"Fuck you. And my sister says your brother's gay."

"Yeah? Well he says she's a right fucking slag."

And then the bell goes and we go to the next lesson. I've gone off Lorna. And her sister is definitely a slag.

For the next few months, we get into a sort of routine, Parthipan, me and Nan. He comes over and pretends to be Egyptian, with the heating turned full up and the joss sticks smoking away, whilst Al Jazeera plays on the telly in the corner and the MP3 player makes busy street sounds. Nan's as happy as I've know her for years. She hasn't a clue what time of day it is, only that she's in Cairo, where she's always wanted to be.

And then one day she doesn't seem to be quite as strong as she once was and I realise that she's been declining for quite some time. All of a sudden she says, "I want to go home." I look at Parthipan and he looks back at me. We nod at each other, and then we quietly turn off the heating, stub out the incense and switch the television and the MP3 player off.

"Want to go to sleep now."

Parthipan holds my hand all the way through the funeral. I glance up every now and then, and there are tears rolling down his cheeks. We give her a lovely send-off, with "Arabian Moods" playing as her coffin rolls into the furnace. It's what she would have wanted.

Afterwards, I get chatting to my Great Aunt Mabel, and I ask her about Nan going to Cairo. She laughs.

"Don't be daft. She never left England." Then she pauses for a moment. "Nah, the nearest she ever got was a cup of tea in the Cairo Café in the old arcade. You're probably too young to remember it, aren't you? Nice little place. Pictures of the pyramids on the walls. Used to do lovely macaroons."

I smile to myself. I guess I knew all along. But you know what? One day I'm going to go to Egypt and see for myself. I like the sound of the place.

www.jonathanpinnock.com
@jonpinnock

I refuse to open my eyes.

Monday morning waking up is never welcome; it presages the need to face another teaching workday. Wild animal management wasn't my career ambition when I trained as a teacher but that's what it's like.

The six-thirty alarm bleats. My arm flails in the air, but misses. My eyes refuse to open so I close my ears to the alarm.

The sound comes from the wrong direction. Perhaps it isn't my wake-up, but Alan's in the apartment above.

As long as I don't open my eyes I won't worry. I shuffle in preparation to roll onto my right side. Whoa, I can't. My back muscles won't cooperate.

At last I open my eyes... and I discover that I am on the ceiling.

...

I laugh. Nerves. Then my stomach knots. I am on the ceiling, looking down. Aren't I? Has Alan re-arranged my room during sleeptime in order to make it appear inverted? The only thing worse than a science teacher is one with a warped sense of humour. I squeeze my eyelids shut then slowly re-open them. Below, covered with an untidy red quilt, is my bed. The bedside cabinet is next to it, supporting the alarm clock, which periodically bursts into indignation at being ignored.

I send my impending terror into an unused lump of brain, a trick learnt when teaching difficult classes.

How can I verify if either the room has turned upside down or it's me? Has a trickster stuck my furniture down? My right arm that had swung into action has returned up to the ceiling. Turning my head, I see the white plaster ceiling-rose. I've not seen my Georgian ceiling this close up. Cracks in the paintwork and plaster missing near the rose remind the few functioning brain cells that I should get workmen in. Banality subjugates fear.

I seek evidence of gravity. Before my mind boils in terror I allow a drop of spittle to go where it will. It accelerates away to the quilt below. A dark red splodge grows like a bloodstain.

Forcing my mind into more experiments, denying the inevitable panic, I turn my head to the left. As I thought from its soft undulations, the pillow remains under, or rather above – all right, behind – my head. Good loyal pillow.

This is absurd. I must be in a nightmare. Nevertheless, perhaps I should exercise caution in any effort to break free from the ceiling's suction force. What if normality returns? I'd fall at an acceleration of ten metres per second each second. Well, it's no more than three metres so a quick calculation tells me I'd land at seventeen miles an hour. Is that fast enough to hurt? My blob of spit must have landed at that speed too. The fall was languorous to me; yet look at what happened to it.

Hopefully, the bed will be kind to my eventual return. The mattress is one of those with memory. It's probably wondering where I am.

I wriggle again. Has Alan velcroed my pyjamas to the ceiling? Even if he had, how did he get a stepladder and manhandle a sleeping adult up to a tall ceiling?

It couldn't be Velcro holding me up. My arms are free but kind of floating. It's like when I go snorkelling: face-down looking at the seabed. It's a strange but pleasant experience in the water, but weird and worrying now. Perhaps my room is full of water.

I look for contrary evidence. On the green carpet, there's a bedtime book, Orbital Geometry. It isn't floating: too heavy. If I'm in water my spittle shouldn't have fallen – unless it isn't normal water.

A worry headache is brewing.

I scan for objects that should float. What is there in a bedroom that should float, besides a person? I assume I'm breathing, aren't I? And the usual air. Now I'm holding my breath wondering if somehow I'm immersed in a highly oxygenated liquid, or perhaps I've not been breathing.

"Am I dead?" I yell realizing instantly that I'd breathed to make the shout.

"No!" A female voice far down the corridor. It sounded like Suzette.

"In here, Suzy, but keep hold of the door frame." I want to tell her to rush around to the garden, fetch the washing line, tie it to her waist and then to the radiator before opening the door, but it would sound too bizarre.

"What did you say?" Her voice becomes louder as she walks down the corridor to the door of my bedroom. As I watch the mock-crystal handle rotate I wouldn't be surprised to find her walking on the ceiling. But no, there's her mass of hazelnut brown hair, far below. She hasn't removed her beige raincoat. Her naked foot steps into the room.

"John, where are you?"

Why hadn't she seen this ceiling person immediately and scream? My panic turns from defiantly off to simmer. How to mention my predicament without freaking her out? I absently cough.

Her face is a picture. The Scream by Edvard Munch comes to mind. I see she's had her teeth whitened recently. I hadn't noticed before.

"What the heck are you doing up there?"

I struggle to answer, but remain silent.

Suzy wags a finger at me. "Get down, you goon."

"Nothing I'd like better. Any suggestions?"

She stands hands on hips, her raincoat unbuttoned at the neck with no visible clothing beneath, the thought wheedles into my head that she may have planned an interesting morning. Damn.

"Why did you go up there?"

Not how?

"I woke up like this." It sounds stupid but then it only confirms the perception she possesses of my propensity for finding myself in odd situations.

"Maybe I can lure you down." She undoes a couple of buttons revealing her cleavage, which translates to part of my anatomy that finally points towards the floor.

"I am lured, but... hey, Suzy, don't climb on the bed. This isn't like the leaping-off-the-wardrobe scenario."

"Idiot, I was seeing if I could reach you."

"You know these old buildings have really high ceilings. And what if you could reach? You could have been seriously injured."

"John, stop all this now."

"It's not much fun for me. Go tell Alan to turn off whatever he's done upstairs."

"What, you think Einstein has invented a man attractor in his apartment and it's sucked you up? How do you know it's not Freya?"

I'd forgotten about Alan's latest oddball woman. "Be careful if you go upstairs and see her, she's quite unpredictable."

"We've met. Freya gave me a bangle at Alan's birthday party last week. It turned my veins green, from my wrist up my arm and down the other one – remember? I'll give Alan a call."

Only when she leaves the room does my nose detect the heady aroma of Freesia. She only wore it for our romantic interludes. In spite of my increasing concern I smile ruefully then frown. It is Monday mid-morning. I should, by now, be edutaining the masses, so why is Suzette here and dressed for action? Who was she expecting, and in my room. Alan? Freya? Both?

I wriggle, but it is as if my lungs are made of iron and a powerful electro-magnet is above the ceiling. Even with both hands pushing, trying to make fists, my back presses firmly upwards. In frustration I bang the ceiling. Mistake. White flakes of plaster wander down messing up my bed. My nose pinches with the musty aroma.

I hear dragging noises. Someone must be moving furniture, a large machine, or is intent on driving me insane. I try to think if I've annoyed Alan recently, or at all. Perhaps someone else. Plenty of parents would be aggrieved at my honest grading of their kid's work. The Wagners, from the time I wrote 'the dawn of legibility in Kevin's handwriting revealed his utter incapacity to spell'? Surely not enough. It must be that mad bitch, Freya.

Then there's Suzy. The teasing raincoat and perfume for someone else.

The front door slams. Suzy must have gone outside to make that call to Alan, but she has a mobile. She must have left it in her car in spite of all my warnings.

Footsteps in the corridor.

"Is that you, Suzette? ... Suzy? ... Freya?"

The door handle moves, and the door cracks open, but then a scuffling noise followed by Suzy's scream.

"What's happened, Suzy?"

I strain harder, trying to arch my back even though it's agony now.

A feeble voice reaches me from the corridor. "John, whatever it is holding you up on the ceiling...?"

"Well?"

"It's spreading."

Index

Other ideas4writers publications

Visit www.ideas4writers.co.uk to find out more.

Need ideas for a new writing project?

We have over 5,000 of them, spanning 35 categories:

Characters, Description and Setting, Dialogue, Plot, Structure, Theme

Fiction, Novels, Plays, Screenplays, Short Stories, Storylines

Comedy, Crime, Erotica, Fantasy, Historical, Horror, Mystery and Suspense, Romance, Science Fiction, Thrillers

Editing, Getting Ideas, Getting Published, Overcoming Rejection, Self-Publishing, Writer's Block, Writing

Magazine Articles, Non-Fiction Books, Poetry,Teens/Young Adult, Travel Writing, Writing for Children

They're all available as ebooks (currently PDF and Kindle) and we're gradually releasing them in paperback and other ebook formats too.

Need newsworthy and notable historic anniversaries months in advance?

We publish a new edition of *The Date-A-Base Book* each year. Each one gives details of over 1,500 notable anniversaries of historic events, discoveries, inventions, famous births and deaths, and more.

Each edition lists anniversaries at least a year in advance, giving you time to choose the ones you'd like to write about, research them, and get your work onto the editor's desk ahead of everyone else.

Several of our regular customers make a full-time living from writing about the anniversaries in these books. They're also used by many of the major media outlets, TV/radio production companies and broadcasters, festival and event organisers, and more.

Our other publications include:

The Fastest Way to Write Your Book

The Fastest Way to Get Ideas: 4,400 Essential What Ifs for Writers

Printed in Great Britain
by Amazon